M000306680

Principles
in Practice

The Principles in Practice imprint offers teachers concrete illustrations of effective classroom practices based in NCTE research briefs and policy statements. Each book discusses the research on a specific topic, links the research to an NCTE brief or policy statement, and then demonstrates how those principles come alive in practice: by showcasing actual classroom practices that demonstrate the policies in action; by talking about research in practical, teacher-friendly language; and by offering teachers possibilities for rethinking their own practices in light of the ideas presented in the books. Books within the imprint are grouped in strands, each strand focused on a significant topic of interest.

Adolescent Literacy Strand

Adolescent Literacy at Risk? The Impact of Standards (2009) Rebecca Bowers Sipe

Adolescents and Digital Literacies: Learning Alongside Our Students (2010) Sara Kajder

Adolescent Literacy and the Teaching of Reading: Lessons for Teachers of Literature (2010) Deborah Appleman

Writing in Today's Classrooms Strand

Writing in the Dialogical Classroom: Students and Teachers Responding to the Texts of Their Lives (2011) Bob Fecho

Becoming Writers in the Elementary Classroom: Visions and Decisions (2011) Katie Van Sluys

Writing Instruction in the Culturally Relevant Classroom (2011) Maisha T. Winn and Latrise P. Johnson

Literacy Assessment Strand

Our Better Judgment: Teacher Leadership for Writing Assessment (2012) Chris W. Gallagher and Eric D. Turley

Beyond Standardized Truth: Improving Teaching and Learning through Inquiry-Based Reading Assessment (2012) Scott Filkins

Reading Assessment: Artful Teachers, Successful Students (2013) Diane Stephens, editor

Literacies of the Disciplines Strand

Entering the Conversations: Practicing Literacy in the Disciplines (2014) Patricia Lambert Stock, Trace Schillinger, and Andrew Stock

Real-World Literacies: Disciplinary Teaching in the High School Classroom (2014) Heather Lattimer

Doing and Making Authentic Literacies (2014) Linda Denstaedt, Laura Jane Roop, and Stephen Best

NCTE Editorial Board

Jamal Cooks
Mary Ellen Dakin
Korina Jocson
Ken Lindblom
Heidi Mills
John Pruitt
Kristen Hawley Turner
Vivian Vasquez
Scott Warnock
Kurt Austin, Chair, ex officio
Kent Williamson, ex officio

Doing and Making Authentic Literacies

Linda Denstaedt
Oakland (MI) Writing Project and
National Writing Project

Laura Jane Roop
University of Pittsburgh and
Western Pennsylvania Writing Project

Stephen Best
Michigan Department of Education

National Council of Teachers of English
1111 W. Kenyon Road, Urbana, Illinois 61801-1096

Staff Editor: Bonny Graham

Series Editor: Cathy Fleischer

Interior Design: Victoria Pohlmann

Cover Design: Pat Mayer

Cover Photo: Linda Denstaedt

NCTE Stock Number: 12199; eStock Number: 12182
ISBN 978-0-8141-1219-9; eISBN 978-0-8141-1218-2

©2014 by the National Council of Teachers of English.

All rights reserved. No part of this publication may be reproduced or transmitted in any form or by any means, electronic or mechanical, including photocopy, or any information storage and retrieval system, without permission from the copyright holder. Printed in the United States of America.

It is the policy of NCTE in its journals and other publications to provide a forum for the open discussion of ideas concerning the content and the teaching of English and the language arts. Publicity accorded to any particular point of view does not imply endorsement by the Executive Committee, the Board of Directors, or the membership at large, except in announcements of policy, where such endorsement is clearly specified.

Every effort has been made to provide current URLs and email addresses, but because of the rapidly changing nature of the Web, some sites and addresses may no longer be accessible.

Library of Congress Cataloging-in-Publication Data

Denstaedt, Linda.
    Doing and making authentic literacies / Linda Denstaedt, Laura Jane Roop, Stephen Best.
        pages cm.
    Includes bibliographical references and index.
    ISBN 978-0-8141-1219-9 (pbk.)
    1. Active learning. 2. Interdisciplinary approach in education. I. Roop, Laura Jane, 1959– II. Best, Stephen, 1969– III. Title.
    LB1027.23.D46 2014
    371.3—dc23
                                                                    2014019369

Contents

Permission Acknowledgments

Page 1: Photo by Meeno courtesy of www.cainesarcade.com. Check out the Global Cardboard Challenge at the Imagination Foundation (http://imagination.is).

Page 41: Photo provided courtesy of University of Michigan College of Engineering/Michigan Sea Grant.

Acknowledgments

We would like to thank the amazing teachers featured in this book—friends and colleagues all—who approach their education work and their life journeys with passion and courage, learning for the sakes of their students. Several featured practitioners in particular have inspired us and challenged our thinking:

- **Bob Moses**, civil rights organizer and founder of the Algebra Project, an outstanding mathematics teacher who has intentionally focused on students in the bottom quartile, particularly students of color and students living in poverty
- **Dick Moscovic** and **Duane Olds**, construction teachers and contractors in Clarkston, Michigan, who have learned how to bring out the best in students too often alienated and disenfranchised in traditional school settings

Their tenacity and depth of commitment left us marveling and pushed us to step up our own efforts on behalf of young people poorly served by current systems.

So many other caring, reflective practitioners also collaborated with us to share their stories and to help us grasp the key aspects of their work. In some cases, young people themselves shared samples of their thinking and writing and offered reflections on the kind of teaching that inspires powerful learning.

Contributing practitioners we'd like to thank include Melanie Depray Learst, Peter Haun, Kathleen Hayes-Parvin, Rick Joseph, Kathleen Kryza, Katie Locano, Laura Mahler, Carissa Peterson, Pauline Roberts, Ann Rzepka, Peter Shaheen, Marcy Sliwinski, Steven Snead, Hans Sowder, James Tuttle, and Bill Woerner.

We'd also like to thank representatives of multiple teacher networks that have shaped our understandings:

- **The National Writing Project** (Joye Alberts, Tanya Baker, Elyse Eidman-Aadahl, and Toby Loftus-Kahn)
- **The Oakland Writing Project** (Leah Barnett, Anne Ruggles Gere, Susan Golab, Richard Koch, Lesley Rex, and Laura Schiller)
- **The Algebra Project** (Greg Budzban, Bill Crombie, Lynne Godfrey, and Ben Moynihan)
- **The Michigan Mathematics and Science Teacher-Leadership Collaborative** (a grant-funded network that lived for about five years in our state)

Special thanks as well to Danielle Lillge, who collaborated and innovated with Linda and the teachers in Oak Park. Her insights and calm resilience were beneficial to all. In addition, we're appreciative of and influenced by research conducted by Arthur Applebee, Bob Bain, Deborah Ball, Judith Langer, Elizabeth Moje, Chauncey Monte-Sano, Fred Newmann, Nichole Pinkard, Walter Secada, and Gary Wehlage.

We're grateful for the encouragement and painstaking help provided by our incredible editor, Cathy Fleischer, and for the editing and proofreading prowess of Bonny Graham and the NCTE team.

For us, a marvelous additional gift has been the deepening of our friendship as we slowed down, looked closely, compared notes, and jointly made sense of the various classroom moments and contexts we've experienced as we tried to convey how teachers traveled toward powerful practice that built student agency.

Literacies *of* Disciplines
An NCTE Policy Research Brief

The Issue

Consider this: Fourth graders in the US score among the highest in the world on literacy assessments, but by tenth grade the same students score among the lowest. We know that the texts read by tenth graders are longer and more complex, demand greater abilities to synthesize information, and present conceptual challenges. All of these features are compounded by the fact that much of the reading done by tenth graders—actually all students beyond the fourth or fifth grade—is grounded in specific disciplines or content areas.[1]

The discrepancy between adolescent readers in the US and their peers elsewhere in the world and the apparent decline in literacy capacities as students move beyond elementary school suggests a problem that needs attention. A first step in addressing this issue is to examine the meanings carried by literacy and disciplines.

Literacies and Disciplines

Research over the past few decades shows that literacy is not a single or monolithic entity. Rather, it is a set of multi-faceted social practices that are shaped by contexts, participants, and technologies. This plurality is reflected in the many ways terms are taken up and used in research on literacy. For example, a survey of studies published in the *Journal of Literacy Research* found a wide range of meanings associated with the term *context*, which suggests that many related terms, including *literacy*, have multiple meanings. The plurality of literacy extends beyond the print-only world of reading and writing to new and developing technologies, along with visual, audio, gestural, spatial, or multimodal discourses. It is much more accurate, then, to adopt a perspective of plurality, to focus on literacies, recognizing the multiple values and meanings along with the ways literacies are inflected by different contexts.[2]

Disciplines is likewise a complicated term. One complication arises from the fact that disciplines, as they are conceived in higher education, do not exist in secondary schools. Content areas or school subjects in secondary schools are organized differently—social studies, for example, does not exist as a discipline although it is a high school subject—and school subjects often operate to constrain or control how knowledge is presented, while disciplines emphasize the creation of knowledge. Furthermore, while it is possible to identify general qualities—problem solving, empirical inquiry, research from sources, and performance—that distinguish academic areas from one another, the boundaries of disciplines are increasingly flexible and porous. No single discipline can function as a rigidly fixed container of knowledge. As Carter (2007) puts it, it is more productive to "emphasize not disjunction but junction, the intersections of disciplines, the connections between research and teaching, and the ties between writing and knowing. From this perspective, the issue is not so much writing in or outside but writing of the disciplines" (410).[3]

Literacies *of* Disciplines

Developing a New Model

Putting literacies next to disciplines adds another layer of complexity. Traditionally literacies and disciplines have come together as teachers have required students to utilize common strategies of reading and writing in each of their content-area classes. Research shows, however, that this approach does not engender student literacies in multiple disciplines. As Moje (2011) explains, "strategies—absent some level of knowledge, a purpose for engaging in the literate practice and an identification with the domain or the purpose—will not take readers or writers very far" (52). Instead, instruction is most successful when teachers engage their students in thinking, reading, writing, speaking, listening, and interacting in discipline-specific ways, where literacies and content are not seen as opposites but rather as mutually supportive and inextricably linked. When put next to literacies, then, disciplines represent unique languages and structures for thinking and acting; disciplines are spaces where students must encounter, be supported in, and be expected to demonstrate a plurality of literacies. This means taking a much more nuanced approach to disciplines and at the same time affirming the plurality of literacies. As such, all teachers play an equally important role because no one class or teacher can best develop students' literacies apart from discipline-informed resources and lenses.[4]

What Are the Benefits of Literacies of Disciplines?

Research shows that when schools create explicit spaces for students and teachers to discuss the overlap and the differences among disciplinary literacies, teachers become more effective, and students develop new ways of representing and generating knowledge. Learning in the discipline is fostered by multiple literacies, and the learning of literacies is likewise expanded. This process, in turn, enables students to traverse and to transfer learning across disciplines—thus enhancing their ability to become learners who make connections and draw distinctions to function more effectively, whether in classrooms or on-the-job.[5]

Classrooms where literacies of disciplines flourish are nurturing environments for formative assessment. The specificity of discipline-based literacies enables teachers and students to focus on only a few issues at a time, an essential feature for formative assessment because it allows teachers to give students the feedback they need to evaluate their own work without imposing grades. Teachers can use formative assessment to shape instruction based on student progress; considering student performance enables teachers to pinpoint areas where students may need more focused teaching. And teachers in specific disciplines are best prepared to assess student literacies in a given field. The processes associated with formative assessment help students relate new concepts to their prior knowledge in any discipline, making them more likely to transfer learning from one context to another.[6]

What Support Do Literacies of Disciplines Need?

Implementing literacies of disciplines will require significant attention to professional development for teachers. Teacher learning is an integral element not just of the teacher's continuing professional education, but also of student achievement. Teachers may learn in varying contexts—through their teaching experiences, school communities, conversations with colleagues, hallway interactions with students, or through professional development opportunities like workshops, inservices, or classes.

Regardless of how they learn, that learning will have a direct effect on what their students are able to accomplish. As the Common Core State Standards (CCSS) are implemented in most states across the nation, new forms of professional development will be required. The CCSS give literacies of disciplines a central position, and teachers will need professional development that addresses how the learning of literacies may be approached within their disciplines.

The professional development that will provide teachers with the resources and strategies necessary to support students in acquiring plural literacies needs to be sustained and systematic because episodic or unfocused learning experiences will not give teachers from multiple disciplines sufficient opportunities for effective learning. One of the most powerful forms of professional development is communities of practice. The National Writing Project exemplifies this approach by bringing together English language arts teachers from multiple schools for an intensive and sustained experience of learning, and research shows that this learning is transformative for teachers and their students. However, for literacies of discipline to flourish, a more cross-disciplinary form of professional development is needed.[7]

How Can We Develop Communities of Practice That Support Literacies of Disciplines?

By working with colleagues from several fields in the context of a long-term intentional community, teachers can become more aware of how their professional knowledge is developed through informal interactions. They can come to see their colleagues as resources for learning, and they can move smoothly between teaching and learning, implementing and reflecting on that implementation with colleagues. They can also gain deeper understandings of disciplinary literacy expectations by reading and discussing publications that address this issue. Experiences like these enable teachers to move beyond thinking of professional development as a one-time event and instead view it as an ongoing, recursive process that improves their own learning across different spaces and contexts. With this kind of professional development, teachers can support students as they learn to explore the multiple literacies of disciplines.[8]

Notes

1. UNESCO Institute for Statistics (2007). Global education digest: Comparing education statistics across the world. Montreal. Retrieved from http://www.uis.unesco.org/template/pdf/ged/2007/EN_web2.pdf

2. Rex, L., Green, J., Dixon, C., & Group, S. B. C. D. (1998). What counts when context counts?: The uncommon "common" language of literacy research. *Journal of Literacy Research, 30*(3), 405–433.

Literacies *of* Disciplines

Russell, D. (2001). Where do the naturalistic studies point? A research review. In S. H. MacLeod, E. Miraglia, M. Soven, & C. Thaiss (Eds.), *WAC for the new millennium: Strategies for continuing writing-across-the-curriculum programs* (pp. 259–325). Urbana: NCTE.

The New London Group. (2000). A pedagogy of multiliteracies: Designing social futures. In B. Cope and M. Kalantzis (Eds.), *Multiliteracies: Literacy learning and the design of social futures* (pp. 9–37). New York: Routledge.

3. Carter M. (2007). Ways of knowing, doing and writing in the disciplines. *College Composition and Communication, 58*(3), 385–418.

Heller, R. (2010). In praise of amateurism: A friendly critique of Moje's "call for change" in secondary literacy. *Journal of Adolescent & Adult Literacy, 54*(4), 267–273.

O'Brien, D. G., Steward, R. A., & Moje, E. B. (1995). Why content area literacy is difficult to infuse into the secondary school: Complexities of curriculum, pedagogy, and school culture. *Reading Research Quarterly, 30*(3), 442–463.

4. Draper, R. J., Broomhead, P., Jensen, A. P., Nokes, J. D., & Siebert, D. (Eds.). (2010). *(Re)imagining content-area literacy instruction.* New York: Teachers College Press & National Writing Project.

Langer, J. A. (2011). *Envisioning knowledge: Building literacy in the academic disciplines.* New York: Teachers College Press.

Moje, E. B. (2008). Foregrounding the disciplines in secondary literacy teaching and learning: A call for change. *Journal of Adolescent & Adult Literacy, 52*(2), 96–107.

Moje, E. B. (2008). Responsive literacy teaching in secondary school content areas. In M. W. Conley, J. R. Freidhoff, M. B. Sherry, & S. F. Tuckey (Eds.), *Meeting the challenge of adolescent literacy: Research we have, research we need* (pp. 58–87). New York: Guilford Press.

Moje, E. B. (2011). Developing disciplinary discourses, literacies and identities: What's knowledge got to do with it? In M. G. L. Bonilla and K. Englander (Eds.) *Discourses and identities in contexts of educational change: Contributions from the United States and Mexico* (49–74). New York: Peter Lang.

5. Bergman, L. S., & Zepernick, J. (2007). Disciplinary transfer: Students' perceptions of learning to write. *Writing Program Administration, 31*(1), 124–149.

Childers, P. B. (2007). High school-college collaborations: Making them work. *Across the Disciplines, 7.*

Graff, N. (2010). Teaching rhetorical analysis to promote transfer of learning. *Journal of Adolescent & Adult Literacy, 53*(5), 376–385.

Thaiss, C., & Zawacki, T. M. (2006). *Engaged writers dynamic disciplines: Research on the academic writing life.* Portsmouth: Heinemann.

Young, A. (2006). *Teaching writing across the curriculum.* Upper Saddle River, NJ: Pearson Prentice Hall.

6. Black, P., & Wiliam, D. (2009). Developing the theory of formative assessment. *Educational Assessment, Evaluation and Accountability, 21*(1), 5–31.

Cauley, K., & McMillan, J. (2010). Formative assessment techniques to support student motivation and achievement. *The Clearing House, 83*(1), 1–6.

Pryor, J., & Croussuard, B. (2008). A socio-cultural theorization of formative assessment. *Oxford Review of Education, 34*(1), 1–20.

7. Borko, H. (2004). Professional development and student learning: Mapping the terrain. *Educational Researcher*, *33*(8), 3–15.

Whitney, A. (2008). Teacher transformation in the National Writing Project. *Research in the Teaching of English*, *43*(2), 44.

8. Grossman, P., Wineburg, S., & Woolworth, S. (2001). Toward a theory of teacher community. *Teacher College Record*, *103*(6), 942–1012.

Moje, E. B. (2008). Foregrounding the disciplines in secondary literacy teaching and learning: A call for change. *Journal of Adolescent and Adult Literacy*, *52*(2), 92–107.

Webster-Wright, A. (2009). Reframing professional development through understanding authentic professional learning. *Review of Educational Research*, *79*(2), 702.

This policy brief was produced by NCTE's James R. Squire Office of Policy Research, directed by Anne Ruggles Gere, with assistance from Elizabeth Homan, Will Hutchinson, Danielle Lillge, Justine Neiderhiser, Sarah Swofford, Crystal VanKooten, all students in the Joint PhD Program in English and Education at the University of Michigan, and Amanda Thompson, a student at the University of Virginia.

Why Move toward Authentic Literacies?

Young people are capable of extraordinary things. At age sixteen, Nikhil Goyal, spurred by his sense that the education system remained "a 19th century factory-based model," began writing op-ed pieces and engaging in public speaking. At seventeen, his book, *One Size Does Not Fit All: A Student's Assessment of School* (2012), was published (see http://nikhilgoyal.me). Malala Yousafzai, a young Pakistani activist who argued that young women deserved quality education as much as young men, was nominated for the International Children's Peace Prize by Desmond Tutu at age thirteen and nominated for the Nobel Peace Prize at sixteen. She now has a popular book out: *I Am Malala: The Girl Who Stood Up for Education and Was Shot by the Taliban* (2013). Finalists, ages thirteen to eighteen, in the global Google Science Fair created a new anti-flu medicine, a battery-free flashlight, and bioplastics made from a banana peel. Two talented Atlanta sisters, Chloe and Halle Bailey, ages fifteen and thirteen, embarked on acting and singing careers and now have a YouTube channel with more than 200,000 subscribers. Several years ago near Los Angeles, nine-year-old Caine Monroy spent a summer building an arcade from cardboard boxes in his father's auto parts store, and when a local filmmaker made a short video of his construction, the video went viral. Currently, almost $250,000 of college funding has been donated on Caine's behalf, and an annual Global Cardboard Challenge has been instituted, involving more than 85,000 people in forty-six countries—and Caine isn't even a teenager yet. On a less lofty note, check out the amazing number of DIY room decorating and book trailer videos now on YouTube generated by adolescents.

What if we were to take advantage of the tremendous potential young people possess, and the "out-of-the-box" thinking they are capable of, to design environments in which all can unleash, develop, and publicly share their talents? Instead of "doing school"—working from textbook-driven, often contrived "school subjects"—what if we aimed for something else with our students, something closer to the public, energized achievements of accomplished adults? In too many cases, we would argue, students aren't seeing themselves as "doers" and "makers," authentically engaged in disciplines, with real prospects for using these lenses for their future lives and work. In some situations, teachers have felt so pressured to engage in coverage of ever-expanding topics and in test preparation that they haven't allotted the time or created the space for youth to experience the exhilaration of trying on adult roles and literate identities as they learn. There is little time for play and experimentation in many schools. But in the age of the Internet, it becomes ever more evident: virtually every accomplished individual plying a trade or working in a profession—from musician to engineer to social worker to scientist—engages in "doing" and "making." They apply their hard-earned knowledge to creation; they make "stuff" ranging from symphonic performances to designs for motor vehicles to plans for strengthening social capital on behalf of struggling families to new methods for generating energy. Professionals do not only "do" and "make," applying the knowledge and skills they've learned to use in order to create. Inevitably, they also communicate, enthusiastically and meaningfully, to various others about these creative acts across a range of modes and media. They experience "flow" (Csikszentmihalyi, 1990)—that state in which a person is so immersed and energized by the task at hand that he or she hardly realizes time is passing.

While the three of us believe wholeheartedly in the need for schools to strive toward authentic doing and making, we've also learned firsthand to attend closely to the development of disciplinary literacies. In fact, we think that for work in classrooms to be truly authentic, students must engage in the actual, rigorous practices of thinking, reading, talking, and creating that exist in every disciplinary subject and are applied in work and citizenship. These practices are foundational, but they really can't be separated from their purposeful uses. What if we were to revise classroom emphases so that young people could see *why* they were learning chemistry or history and *how* they could actively apply their learning, stepping into the space as apprentices in a grown-up world? What if the power of the extracurriculum—sports competitions, musicals, science fairs, and comic book clubs, all happening after school, on weekends, and in summers, as a few examples—was leveraged for all students during the school day? What if new forms, such as "maker spaces" and "DIY clubs," were recognized as places where both literacies and identities are built? Mightn't it make a big difference in students' levels of engagement and achievement? Mightn't it lead to the strengthening of students' sense that they are people who can use their talents and their voices to change our world for the better—with no need to wait until adulthood?

Who We Are

As authors of this book, we (Linda Denstaedt, Laura Roop, and Steve Best) believe there is a traceable path toward this vision of authentic literacy. Our task in writing this book is to outline concrete steps along the way and render them "learnable" by others. For the three of us, growing interest in and commitment to understanding authentic learning and the role of disciplinary literacies has shaped our teaching practice and our professional learning trajectories. Two of us (Linda and Laura), English teachers by training, went into the profession believing in the power of authentic work. Laura had the good fortune to have a writing workshop teacher in high school for creative writing and journalism, so when she became a teacher, she pictured her students publishing newspapers and magazines and giving readings of their work, just as she had. Over the years, though, she has realized that there are additional skills educators need to develop to deepen their understandings of disciplines and fields and to create opportunities for students to share their work publicly and to build the partnerships needed to push school cultures and systems away from a nineteenth-century model. Directing a National Writing Project (NWP) site, Laura also learned that, when working with practicing teachers in various subjects, generic strategies in reading and writing don't get us very far. For the last six years, she has been collaborating with mathematics teachers, mathematicians, and other educators from the Algebra Project, a national education improvement network, aimed at learners in the bottom quartile.

Linda shifted her view on teaching and learning after she connected with the Oakland Writing Project (OWP), an affiliate of the National Writing Project, in an effort to become a better teacher of writing. Her experience in OWP led her to create a poetry portfolio and submit it for admission to the Vermont Studio Center, a residential community for artists and writers of all genres. There, she worked with poets Stephen Dunn and Robert Pinsky. When she returned to her classroom, student and teacher talk changed. Although she had previously incorporated cooperative learning protocols for talk and writer response groups, she now began talking to students the way professional writers had talked to her—as a fellow writer—and she encouraged her students to see themselves as writers and to write for publication beyond school. Every student submitted work; some were published or won competitions. Eventually, Linda designed and facilitated the Communication Arts Center in her school that supported the creation and implementation of high school teacher and student learning in project-based, authentic disciplinary work. For example, a social studies teacher wanted to learn how to write editorials and to create a unit so his students would be able to submit editorials to a local newspaper's competition, while a teacher of Japanese wanted to understand the software technology as well as the elements of storytelling so that her students could create digital animated stories told in Japanese. Most recently, Linda conducted ethnographic research in a construction trades classroom to understand how the instructional practices of an authentic learning environment impacts student identities and agency. She applied this learning as she worked as an embedded consultant and coach in a low-performing high school. Working side by side with teachers and students transitioning from textbooks to authentic literacies, Linda also learned that attention to student identities is key, regardless of the disciplinary context.

Steve, a mathematics and science teacher by training, began introducing authentic reading and writing through academic projects to enhance student understandings and connections to science and mathematics. While he recognized the need to develop these skills in authentic discourse for his students, it wasn't until he became immersed in one of these projects, a solar car design project, that he specifically began collaborating with both writing experts and disciplinary partners in materials and electrical engineering to foster authentic literacies. This work was the catalyst for his subsequent efforts to engage other teachers in authentic disciplinary investigations with their students on a range of topics, including ecological and environmental protection, materials design, civil and architectural engineering, energy systems, and climate change research. Through these activities, Steve recognized that teachers could not understand this engagement without participating in such efforts collaboratively themselves. Therefore, his workshops and design work with teachers involved the creation of collaborative project design activities that used lesson study as a means to engage multiple teachers in design and action research on authentic disciplinary studies within their own classrooms.

Individually and together, we have learned that a collaborative, interdisciplinary stance is necessary in growing our understandings of authentic learning and literacies in the disciplines. What's more, we've learned that we must think hard about how to consciously structure and offer opportunities for authentic application of disciplinary reading, writing, speaking, listening, and representing—otherwise, we haven't sufficiently considered students' motivation and identity development. We've merely tweaked a model that is leaving far too many young people behind.

NCTE Policy Research Brief on Literacies of Disciplines

In the fall of 2011, the National Council of Teachers of English (NCTE) published a policy research brief on disciplinary literacies. The brief argues for a "much more nuanced approach to disciplines" (p. 16) and for the affirmation of "the plurality of literacies." The brief also notes that "the boundaries of disciplines are increasingly flexible and porous" (p. 15) but that there are ways to "identify general qualities—problem solving, empirical inquiry, research from sources, and performance—that distinguish academic areas from one another." This research brief, which is reprinted in the front matter of this book on pages xi–xv,[1] is part of the impetus that led us to develop the framework behind this book.

> ### The Benefits of Literacies of Disciplines
>
> Students
>
> - Develop ways to represent and generate knowledge
> - Transfer prior knowledge
> - Become learners who solve problems
> - Engage with discipline-specific language
> - Focus on a few issues at a time
> - Receive feedback throughout the learning experience

Like many involved in teaching literacy, we were steeped in "writing across the curriculum" and "reading in the content areas" before our understandings began to evolve in response to what we saw as we partnered with teachers and faculty in diverse disciplines. We were excited to see NCTE colleagues embracing a new angle on literacy—one that digs deeply into particular literacies and emphasizes using reading, writing, speaking, listening, and viewing to take action in specific contexts, engaging with issues and problems of particular subjects as well as in the world more broadly. The research brief led us to heighten our attention to the diverse contexts in which we have been working and to ask ourselves whether we might have something to contribute to a larger conversation.

Why Shift to a Disciplinary Literacies Model?

Back when we entered the profession, the terms du jour were *writing across the curriculum* and *reading in the content areas*. And in fact, for almost forty years our professions have invested in the concepts of writing across the curriculum and reading in the content areas—the former initially in colleges and universities and the latter in K–12 settings and eventually K–college. Typically what people have meant by these terms is the intentional incorporation of informal writing into subjects and lessons, or the explicit teaching of particular strategies in reading or writing, all with the intention of strengthening student understandings. The pioneers of writing across the curriculum, including James Britton (1970), Anne Berthoff (1981, 1984), Toby Fulwiler (1987), Art Young (Young & Fulwiler, 1986), and Anne Gere (1985), have made valuable contributions to literacy learning. The pioneers of reading in the content areas, including Richard Allington (1980, 1983a, 1983b, 2006), Annemarie Palincsar (1982; Palincsar & Brown, 1984), P. David Pearson (Pearson & Fielding, 1991; Pearson & Gallagher, 1983; Pearson & Johnson, 1978), and Michael Pressley (Pressley & Afflerbach, 1995; Pressley et al., 1994; Pressley et al., 1992), have also contributed mightily to our understandings. In particular, at colleges and universities, where students' literacies have been measured at point of admission, the disciplinary focus in departments, along with a host of performances, presentations, research projects, clubs, and teams, makes the study and enactment of writing across the curriculum and reading across the content areas fairly fruitful. Faculty have found that by adding quick-writes to stimulate student thinking, and by having students think carefully about formats, audiences, and purposes, students can deepen their understandings of various topics in measurable ways. And university administrators have supported faculty in this pursuit by establishing writing centers, where both students and faculty can further pursue their literacy questions.

We would argue, however, that within secondary schools writing across the curriculum and reading in the content areas have had a more superficial impact on teaching and learning across that same time frame. The professional development opportunities that have accompanied school or district inquiries have often been too generic or too superficial to make much of a difference in student learning, and the reasons for writing and reading in mathematics, chemistry, history, and the like have often been driven by state testing mandates—a far cry from authenticity. Too often initiatives have operationalized writing across the curriculum and reading in the content areas as "one size fits all." Hence, we've seen school improvement plans that introduce one strategy to the entire school and require all teachers to implement it without nuance, regardless of content area or years of experience teaching. We've also been involved with schools and districts that have claimed to be pursuing reading in the content areas or writing across the curriculum, but that pursuit has been limited to a couple of professional development sessions and meetings over the course of a school year or two. In one relatively affluent district, we witnessed the establishment of a high-tech, interdisciplinary high school writing center, which, after making good headway for four or five years, was disbanded when the district hit a rocky patch financially. And too often, teachers and administrators aren't really looking deeply into the issues that struggling students are facing or aren't accepting that there really is a need to teach disciplinary ways of reading and writing as part of the actual substance of subject area classes.

Perhaps because we have witnessed and participated in so many lackadaisical or short-sighted efforts, we began to question their efficacy. We saw how many practitioners would apply a new strategy they had learned without necessarily thinking through its appropriateness. Elizabeth Moje, a colleague of ours, articulates the limitation of a strategy approach: "[S]trategies—absent some level of knowledge, a purpose for the literate practice and an identification with the domain or the purpose—will not take readers or writers very far" (2011, p. 52).

Our observations have been confirmed recently by Applebee and Langer's national study of writing instruction, conducted in five states from 2008 to 2011. We were part of the research team collecting data in Michigan. Applebee and Langer found that while writing may be occurring a bit more frequently in disciplinary classrooms than it did thirty years ago, and while writing instruction and scaffolding in tasks has grown more sophisticated, its incorporation has not necessarily been transformative for schools or for student learning. Students still spend relatively little time engaged in actual writing, and when they do, it is often timed writing in response to prompts, filling in blanks, or copying (Applebee & Langer, 2011).

In the 2012 article "What Is Disciplinary Literacy and Why Does It Matter?," Timothy Shanahan and Cynthia Shanahan explain a difference they see between content area reading and disciplinary literacy. Content area reading "emphasizes techniques that a novice might use to make sense of a disciplinary text (like how to study a history book for an exam), while disciplinary literacy emphasizes the unique tools that the experts in a discipline use to participate in the work of that discipline" (p. 8). Shanahan and Shanahan trace the roots of disciplinary literacy to content area reading, studies of expert readers, and functional linguistics. As National Writing Project–influenced folks, we would add studies of expert writers and writing across the curriculum to our sense of the roots of "disciplinary literacies." For us, disciplinary literacies are an aspect of the larger push toward authentic learning that can transfer from a school setting to a larger world.

The efforts of Nichole Pinkard and the Digital Youth Network in Chicago have generated a philosophical framework and curricular model that can provide inspiration about a sensible direction as we journey toward authenticity. Pinkard's Digital Urban Youth curriculum model is designed to engage urban youth in authentic roles in goal-based scenarios that provide multiple pathways to new media literacies. She contrasts the public clarity of the pathway to accomplishment in basketball with the opacity of routes to other, equally interesting futures—graphic arts, cinematography, or game design:

> [T]hose wishing to be good point guards understand that they need to learn to drib-
> ble, shoot, and pass the ball while students focused on becoming good centers know
> they need to learn to post up, defend the basket, and rebound. Once students develop
> some of these abilities, they recognize that they must be able to read the floor, run
> plays, and predict opponents' actions. . . . However, if we were to ask a group of
> young people from the inner city about the roles or developmental stages of becoming
> a graphic artist, recording engineer, cinematographer, or game designer, most would
> not have a realistic picture in mind. (Digital Youth Network, n.d.)

Pinkard's Digital Youth Network initiative focuses on communication arts and
begins to map out the terrain we might all work as we begin to design programs
developing the needed literacies—during and after the school day—as young
people step into authentic tasks and roles tied to career and citizenship.

Other Research Supporting This Shift

For us, NCTE's *Literacies* of *Disciplines* policy research brief echoes the call for
deeper, more authentic academic work in secondary schools that has been long-
standing in our careers. One of the most important contributions to this call and
major influences in our work in the late 1990s was a framework developed by Fred
Newmann, Walter Secada, and Gary Wehlage while they were part of the University of Wisconsin Center on Organization and Restructuring of Schools. In the
early nineties, Newmann and Wehlage (1993) described five standards associated
with authentic pedagogy: (1) higher-order thinking, (2) depth of knowledge, (3)
connectedness to the world beyond the classroom, (4) substantive conversation,
and (5) social support for student achievement. In another important work, *A Guide
to Authentic Instruction and Assessment: Vision, Standards, and Scoring* (1995), Newmann, Secada, and Wehlage argued for assessing the quality of intellectual work
students were experiencing in K–12 schooling according to three main criteria: (1)
student construction of knowledge, (2) disciplined inquiry, and (3) value beyond
the classroom. This framework has been used by practitioners and education
researchers to assess the level of tasks assigned, the level of instruction offered, and
the level of student thinking and performance in schools and classrooms. And more
recently, through the Center for Authentic Intellectual Work (http://centerforaiw
.com/aiw-framework-and-research), the framework has been used to design job-
embedded professional learning.

Newmann and colleagues (1993, 1995) were on to something important
when they identified and pressed for the implementation of this framework. The
school districts we worked with in the 1990s that were studying the framework and
considering standards for quality work were, in our experience, making positive
gains before the twin juggernauts of standards-based tests and the No Child Left

Behind law swept through, crushing much thoughtful work and discussion in their wake. We believe it makes sense to return to that sensible work and use it, along with other interesting contributions, revising for the twenty-first century.

For us, Newmann and colleagues (1993, 1995) established a foundation that opened conversations among teachers about what authentic learning looked like and sounded like. Their framework provided a set of lenses for designing and evaluating tasks, practices, and student work. And this enabled us and our teacher partners to begin to see that there are differences in the ways disciplines read, write, think, and inquire. Disciplinarity matters. We could no longer provide a one-size-fits-all fix for all disciplines. When we read NCTE's policy research brief, we saw an opportunity to connect these ideas to the conversation on disciplinarity. Building on these sources, we offer five concrete steps on a journey to understand and engage students in disciplinary inquiries and experiences. The graphic in Figure 1.1 illustrates the relationship of Newmann and colleagues (1993, 1995)

Figure 1.1. The road to authentic literacies.

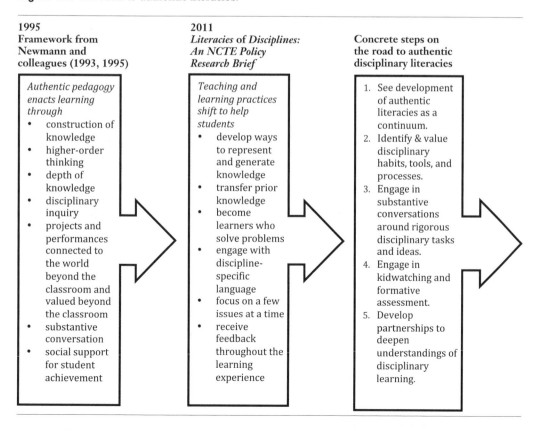

1995 Framework from Newmann and colleagues (1993, 1995)	2011 *Literacies* of *Disciplines: An NCTE Policy Research Brief*	Concrete steps on the road to authentic disciplinary literacies
Authentic pedagogy enacts learning through • construction of knowledge • higher-order thinking • depth of knowledge • disciplinary inquiry • projects and performances connected to the world beyond the classroom and valued beyond the classroom • substantive conversation • social support for student achievement	*Teaching and learning practices shift to help students* • develop ways to represent and generate knowledge • transfer prior knowledge • become learners who solve problems • engage with discipline-specific language • focus on a few issues at a time • receive feedback throughout the learning experience	1. See development of authentic literacies as a continuum. 2. Identify & value disciplinary habits, tools, and processes. 3. Engage in substantive conversations around rigorous disciplinary tasks and ideas. 4. Engage in kidwatching and formative assessment. 5. Develop partnerships to deepen understandings of disciplinary learning.

and NCTE's policy research brief to the concrete steps on the road to authentic disciplinary literacies.

Contexts We Are Drawing On

In writing this book, the three of us—Linda, Laura, and Steve—draw on the kind of thinking just discussed about disciplinary literacies and authentic academic work. Equally important, though, are the amazing opportunities we have had, as professional developers, coaches, and teacher-researchers, to spend years in secondary classrooms in multiple subjects. We've learned so much from observing, coaching, and co-facilitating. Several important local contexts have shaped our thinking about what classrooms might look like if we were to place a premium on "making" and "doing" disciplines.

Construction

One of the most influential contexts has been the construction work sites of Dick Moscovic and Duane Olds, two teachers in metropolitan Detroit. As they have worked with Linda over six years to strengthen and make explicit and intentional students' learning of discourse practices in construction, we came to appreciate the concrete, tangible nature of workshop elements in construction teaching and the cognitive dissonance for us as teachers of academic disciplines. Duane and Dick are definitely doers and makers; they worked on their first construction crews at the age of seventeen. One became a carpenter; one became a mason. Subsequently, they went on to college, became secondary teachers, and, simultaneously, became owners of construction companies. The students working with Duane and Dick literally construct or rehabilitate houses on behalf of Lighthouse International, Grace Centers of Hope, Rebuilding Together, Waterford Township Community Development, and the city of Auburn Hills, Michigan, as part of their coursework.

In the context of the construction site, the students are applying mathematics, reading, writing, and other literacies while engaging in rough carpentry, masonry, painting, landscaping, and more. The abstract ideas of geometry take on a sudden power and significance when the roof of a house is improperly framed. Students in Dick and Duane's classrooms are *doing the discipline* or, more accurately, *doing the applied field* using skills, strategies, habits of action, habits of mind and conversation that construction tradespeople use. They are acting *as* construction tradespeople. Strikingly, many of the students at these construction work site classrooms have not succeeded in more conventional school settings. Something magical is going on as the work plans they generate become actual staircases and houses. The stakes are high, but very real.

Mathematics

Two other settings that have sparked our imaginations were influenced by the Algebra Project, a national network that has spent thirty years determining what mathematics to teach and how to teach it so that struggling students, especially students of color and students living in poverty, can learn it deeply and powerfully. The first setting was Algebra Project founder and civil rights organizer Bob Moses's secondary mathematics classroom laboratory, where he worked with struggling ninth graders for two weeks over three summers at the University of Michigan's School of Education. The second setting was the high school classroom of James Tuttle, who observed in Bob's mathematics laboratory, participated in Algebra Project professional development, and enacted its curricular materials with his Ypsilanti high school students. Both classrooms—James's high school classroom and Bob's highly documented lab classroom—have helped us begin to learn what authentic mathematical work and talk can look like.

In her role as outreach director for the University of Michigan (UM) School of Education, Laura was part of a team that planned student trips, presentations, and summer institutes for the students in James's classroom and in the mathematics laboratory over the course of five years while conducting research, so she had incredible opportunities to observe teaching and planning, to listen to students learning, and even to "do the math" using Algebra Project materials.

English

Multiple English language arts classrooms—connected to our local National Writing Project site, the Oakland Writing Project—have influenced our thinking: the high school classroom of Laura Mahler in Clarkston, Michigan, and the Oak Park High School Department of English in Oak Park, Michigan, among others. Laura Mahler's Advanced Placement (AP) English program has threaded opportunities for serious aesthetic writing toward publication with analytical reading and preparation for the AP assessment. Laura argues that without a fairly substantive "writerly" understanding of literary works, students aren't well positioned to engage in the kind of focused critical writing the exam calls for. For the last three years, Oak Park High School (OPHS) English teachers, as well as teachers from other disciplines at the high school, have been experimenting with Literacy Lab, an effort to infuse reading and writing across disciplines using Smart Boards and complex texts. They've also been conducting teacher inquiries and engaging in Reading Apprenticeship training, all with the aim of improving student outcomes at their school.

Multidisciplinary Teams

Grades 5 and 6 Team: English Language Arts, Social Studies, Mathematics, and Science

Yet another classroom that inspires us to understand the potential of taking authentic doing to its logical extreme is that of our Oakland Writing Project colleague and friend Rick Joseph and his teaching partner, Pauline Roberts. These two Birmingham, Michigan, teachers, who team-teach in grades 5 and 6, recently won an international prize and traveled to Poland to present their "sciracy"—scientific literacy—project, Doing Business in Birmingham. Students inquired into environmental sustainability and then began a campaign to get local businesses to adopt more sustainable practices. Working in teams, they created brochures and a Web-based honor roll, eventually cold-calling nearly every business in their town.

Grade 11 New Tech Team: Science (Chemistry), English Language Arts, and Social Studies

We have been significantly influenced by the team of Ypsilanti New Tech chemistry teacher Melanie Depray Learst and English and social studies teacher Marcy Sliwinski, who partnered with former New Tech teacher Hans Sowder and his colleagues from the UM College of Engineering to co-develop and pilot a study of climate change as viewed through several disciplinary lenses and multiple competing arguments. Actually, the New Tech network, model, and specific local enactment are inspiring in and of themselves; New Tech is an innovative small school design that promotes collaboration; cross- and interdisciplinarity; project-based, one-to-one learning; and the structuring of an environment that encourages professionalism and character development. This national network includes schools in California, Texas, Indiana, Ohio, and Michigan. Marcy and Melanie, who recently became an interdisciplinary team, stepped right into the challenge of co-developing and piloting a study on climate change in collaboration with a team of scientists and engineers who were in the process of building new, more accurate climate impact models for the Great Lakes.

Other practitioners and school staffs are featured in this book as well. Without collaboration and partnership with everybody whose work is discussed here, this book couldn't have been written. The teachers, teams, and school staffs featured are not "perfect" practitioners but instead are learning, growing teachers who sometimes face big problems and sudden changes in circumstances that make their best intentions hard to enact. Some of these teachers have attained certification from the

National Board for Professional Teaching Standards; all are recognized by their peers for their dedication, thoughtfulness, and deep commitment to learning for the sakes of their students. We honor their voices, struggles, questions, and triumphs.

Practices on the Road to Authentic Literacies

As we have worked with these teachers in their diverse settings and subject matter contexts, we've noted four key teaching and learning practices that cut across the disciplines to engage students in powerful learning: (1) constructing opportunities for authentic work, (2) fronting disciplinary lenses, (3) creating opportunities for disciplinary talk, and (4) engaging in formative assessment along the way. We've also identified one crucial professional practice, partnering, that is the foundation on which educational improvement is built.

Chapter 2, "Constructing Opportunities for Authentic Work," introduces an important question we have learned to ask and a continuum of authentic disciplinary literacies that can be used to examine unit, project, or program plans. We look closely at two classrooms well on the way to authentic disciplinary learning. Authentic work requires us to design real-world work spaces and to assess the opportunities we provide: are we developing usable expertise that can be deployed with relation to new problems or projects? As a result of such experiences, students can enact performances closer to those of disciplinary experts, with fluent retrieval of content knowledge as well as broader structural knowledge of disciplinary concepts, decision making, problem solving, and self-monitoring and regulating of processes and social norms (National Research Council, 2000).

Chapter 3, "Fronting Disciplinary Lenses," illustrates a second important teaching and learning strategy. Think of putting on a pair of tinted glasses: a disciplinary lens "tint" would be the habits of mind, the tools, and the intellectual framework of a particular discipline. In this chapter, we explore vignettes from mathematics and science to discuss some of the essential aspects to consider and some of the complications that must be navigated along the road. We compare and contrast two science classrooms where both teachers are trying to front disciplinarity, but one teacher is able to come closer to authenticity.

Chapter 4, "Creating Opportunities for Disciplinary Talk," introduces a third teaching and learning practice: creating spaces for disciplinary talk. It has been said, "Whoever is doing the talking is doing the learning." However, it could also be said, "Whoever is doing the talking has the power." In this chapter, we examine the role of informal, working talk as it occurs in various disciplinary classrooms where students are engaged in "doing the discipline" or "applying knowledge in a field." We demonstrate how teachers working toward authenticity learn to position students as disciplinary knowers through language and role. We also illustrate how teachers can design opportunities for meaningful talk around disciplinary tasks, such as "turn and talk" partnerships, writer response groups, and mathematical explanations.

In Chapter 5, "Engaging in Formative Assessment along the Way," we explore assessment as a dynamic process occurring in the midst of disciplinary instruction that enables learners to move from what they know to what they are able to do next. *Formative assessment* can be defined as a repertoire of information-providing strategies demonstrated through research to have a strong impact on student learning. In our experience, however, such strategies must be nested in a joint, engaged conversation between students and teachers that is integrated in a larger cultural shift in classrooms and schools.

Chapter 6 describes a professional practice that we have come to regard as foundational to teaching growth: partnering for learning. Teaching in a rapidly changing world, with so many forces influencing practice, from new technologies to new policies, may seem virtually impossible unless you build a network of relationships and friendships that help you both keep up and weather the storm. This chapter focuses on the kind of partnering that practitioners must do to move into the kind of deep work that is essential if students are to leave high school with a set of real literacies and learning strategies useful in work and citizenship.

Nikhil Goyal, the young man with whom we began this chapter, urges us in *One Size Does Not Fit All: A Student's Assessment of School*, to change how we do school: "Let's shift classrooms into 'lifelong learning incubators'—student centered and well networked with a level of spontaneity" (2012, Chapter 1). As a young man who has found conventional school tedious and out of touch with the learning he has experienced elsewhere, he asks, "Why are school and life distinguishable? The world should be our school" (Introduction). On behalf of all young people, let's answer Nikhil Goyal's call by stepping down the road to more authentic literacies.

Chapter Two

Constructing Opportunities for Authentic Work

[S]ome of the power of knowledge comes from being an active part of its production rather than from merely possessing it.
—Elizabeth Moje, "Developing Socially Just Subject-Matter Instruction"

The point of school is not to get good at school but to effectively parlay what we learned in school in other learning and life.
—Grant Wiggins, "Transfer as the Point of Education"

What is authentic disciplinary work in a classroom? We would define it as situating students as experts while they construct new knowledge and create a product or performance. The definition seems simple until you unpack the phrases "situating students as experts" and "construct new knowledge." Exactly what do these phrases mean?

In authentic disciplinary learning experiences, students take on particular roles and responsibilities that give them decision-making power and at the same time demand accountability. Once students are given and take on these roles and responsibilities, they are treated like experts even as they develop expertise across time. For instance, Oak Park English teachers Peter Haun and Katie Locano call their high school students "memoirists" even though they are studying and writing memoir for the first time, and they urge their students to make choices about what and how to write. As students enact this role, they use the habits and processes experts use in similar disciplinary work. Memoirists write, rewrite, abandon, and start again to dig deeper into the meaning and importance of an event or series of events. Likewise, Katie's and Peter's students learn to trust the process and not be overly concerned about quality in early writing. Once a teacher puts students into the position of creating something for an audience beyond school, the students must participate actively in a disciplinary community. In Peter's and Katie's classrooms, students imagine, draft, revise, edit, and eventually submit their memoirs to *Teen Ink* and other online publications. The actions, products, or performances they generate become vehicles for the construction of knowledge and expertise. As the teacher takes on the role of coach or thinking partner, students develop agency and independence.

For example, replacing the conventional five-paragraph essay on a whole-class novel with a book review on an independent novel can move students several steps into an authentic learning experience. First, the role shifts from student to book reviewer. And this shift expects that students learn (1) the craft and structural decisions used in the authentic genre of book reviews, (2) the publishing standards and formats for submitting work, and (3) the ways they might read the novel to build an argument about the reasons to recommend a novel. Second, the audience changes—the teacher is no longer the single reader of the essay. Instead, students submit the review to a place like Goodreads. Students now must consider a range of readers: the editors who may accept and publish the submission and the readers of these publications who will gain information and possibly be persuaded to read the book. The more authentic task of writing a book review offers students the opportunity to join a community of fellow readers and book reviewers.

The Authenticity Test

A simple test can become the beginning of a journey toward engagement in authentic classroom work. Here's a question we have used to revise our own practice that can sometimes be used to test our teaching plans: *Is this practice or strategy something that an adult, experienced, literate person really does in the world outside of school?* And if the practice or strategy passes this little test, here is a follow-up question: *Do the students understand its authenticity?* The questions call out two priorities: (1) the practice is used outside of school and (2) students understand how and why it is a literate habit of experienced adults. So let's try out the authenticity test on several teacher assignments (see Figure 2.1).

Figure 2.1. The authenticity test.

Assignment	Used Outside of School	How and Why Used by Experienced Adults
Before writing personal narratives, students write daily entries in a writer's notebook so students capture and explore events, images, ideas, and stories that emerge in daily living.	**Yes.** Some committed writers do keep writing notebooks on almost a daily basis. However, notebooks are just one way to record thoughts and experiences. Experienced writers set their own purposes and uses. Some writers don't use notebooks at all.	Video clips in which YA authors talk about their notebooks; quoted passages in which known writers explain how and why they use notebooks; articles by writers discussing the practice
Before a study of biological cell function, create a K-W-L chart. Return to the chart throughout the study.	**Sometimes.** Some adults do follow the pattern of thinking represented by a K-W-L chart: What do I already know about this topic? What do I want to learn? What did I learn? However, users outside of school may not make a chart and may have more questions than can be tracked by a chart, such as, How will I proceed? How can I keep track of what I am learning?	Interviews or video clips of scientists explaining how the scientific process of inquiry works and how they use the process to begin or extend research to deepen or generate new knowledge about an aspect of cell function
While studying a period of history, write answers to questions at the end of a chapter in a history textbook.	**No.** This activity is something done only in school in order to check the students' comprehension of a text created only for people in school.	

While we aren't saying that teachers should never develop or assign tasks that have no corollary in the world outside of school, we do believe that such school-based tasks should be considered as steps toward the development of authentic disciplinary skills, strategies, and literate habits; and that school-based tasks should be embedded in larger projects or initiatives that make authentic applicability and usefulness clear. By putting tasks and experiences to the authenticity test, teachers can begin to find aspects of schooling that are ripe for reimagination.

Authentic Disciplinary Work: Situating Students as Experts

Dick Moscovic and Duane Olds, Construction Trades
Oakland Schools Technical Campus Northwest

Partnerships: Local Network: Oakland Schools
Technical Campuses; State Network: Michigan
Construction Trades Association (MCTA); Regional
Network: Oakland Writing Project (OWP); Commu-
nity Partnerships: City of Auburn Hills–Hawkwoods
Nature Center, The Well, Grace Centers of Hope,
etc.

The Construction Trades Two-Year Program was one of the most authentic disciplinary learning experiences we studied. Led by Dick Moscovic and Duane Olds,
this program in carpentry and masonry introduces students to knowledge, skills,
and dispositions of the construction trades. As we mentioned in the last chapter,
Dick and Duane work collaboratively with Linda, in her role as co-director of the
local writing project, to design reading and writing units. A typical unit in the program contains routine problem-solving tasks, measuring and ordering tasks typical
of specific stages of construction, as well as brief readings from authentic texts written for a construction tradesperson or home improvement enthusiast.

One of the primary literacy strategies of the unit is use of the construction
notebook, an artifact that follows the construction pathway of the house. Over
time, Dick and Duane noticed that the construction notebook shifted students'
attitudes toward reading and writing. More important, they noticed that through
the notebook students increased their recall of information and their professional
language use onsite. Construction, like other disciplines and applied fields, has a
large content vocabulary that students use to talk about the work and do the work
accurately. If students are framing a wall, they quickly learn the differences between header, king, trimmer, and crippler studs, which serve different purposes.
In construction, content vocabulary translates to accurate and thoughtful product
development.

In addition to helping Dick and Duane develop reading and writing units,
Linda engaged in ethnographic research to understand the instructional practices
at play in their classrooms. On a 9° Fahrenheit February morning during the first
year, she learned how to frame a house alongside fifteen young men who had never
built a house. The experience deepened her understanding of life-changing learning and introduced her to a young man named David.

David, a senior in high school, explained in an interview[2] that he had moved to his father's house and a new school in November of his junior year because he was flunking almost every class. He took construction trades because he hated being in a classroom. But things changed for him his junior year when he worked on a team to build a house in the Construction Trades program. He stopped skipping and he did his homework. In his senior year, his grades improved to As and Bs. As a senior, David split his schedule between his home high school and Oakland Schools Technical Campus Northwest. He took English and social studies in the morning and then drove thirty minutes to the construction trades onsite classroom.

As a senior, David was a team leader. He saw himself as an expert and knower of the multiple literacies required of a construction tradesperson: knowledgeable use of a wide range of tools, certifications in safety and construction mathematics, knowledge of state building code, accurate and efficient product development in rough and finish carpentry, insulation, roofing, siding, and masonry, as well as speaking and listening to clients and co-workers—to name just a few.

If you followed David through his day, the concrete difference between doing school and doing the discipline would be evident. Here is the story of one school day for David during his senior year.

First Hour—Senior English

David arrived as the bell rang and walked silently to a front seat. Shortly after the bell, Mr. Baker invited a student to share her autobiography written as a pictorial PowerPoint. Students watched as she clicked through slides telling her life story. David watched for a brief time and then began reading *Brave New World* to finish his homework, several chapters of which were due that day. Several other students watched briefly but started reading the novel as well.

Next the English teacher facilitated an in-context vocabulary lesson in which students read aloud short passages from *Brave New World* that defined the vocabulary words assigned as homework. Like most students, David followed along in his book as several students offered the meanings of words. Mr. Baker gave other students the page number where the in-context definition was located, and they found and read the passage and then defined the word. If students needed additional support, the teacher explained how the context helped a reader define the word. A young man in the back row drew an intricate video game character on his notebook. Next to him, a young woman held her phone under her desk as she wrote a text message.

Mr. Baker launched into a lecture recommending *Brave New World* as science fiction that provides a critical view of society. Clearly, he loved to read and hoped his students would find joy in reading science fiction novels. Then a young man in the front row asked a question that began a one-to-one conversation as the teacher compared *Brave New World* to several other science fiction novels that critiqued society. Texting and doodling increased during the conversation. David tried to look interested but after several minutes he began to fidget and page through his book.

After the conversation, Mr. Baker announced it was time for independent reading. David spoke briefly to a young man behind him before he began reading. The young man put his head down and went to sleep. Twenty-two students read, pausing to complete questions on the study guide. Two young women opened their books and started a barely audible conversation across the aisle behind their books. David read and wrote answers to the questions even when the other students around him stopped and talked in low voices. He continued reading even when the number of conversations in the room increased. Five minutes before the end of the class, the students shut their books, packed their backpacks, and waited for the bell.

Second Hour—Social Studies

David took a multiple-choice test on a chapter in his textbook.

P.M. Session—Construction Trades Onsite

David began his routine onsite by walking up the driveway and shaking hands with Dick Moscovic, the instructor the students call Coach. Coach asked him about his drive and then assigned him the role of team leader on reconstruction of the porch. As they walked toward the porch, Coach explained that David had an opportunity for problem solving. The morning crew had cut the balusters for the porch railing incorrectly, and there was also a problem with spacing. David's challenge was to correct the situation so it met code. Coach added, "Today is your turn to be a coach, not a criticizer. Remember, they're rookies." He charged David with the task of creating a work plan and asked him to check back before any installation started. David walked to a file box on a makeshift table in the driveway that contained construction notebooks.

David sorted through the box, grabbed his folder, cleared a spot on the table, and read today's task: write a step-by-step plan. Then he took measurements of the railing and porch and returned to his notebook and wrote the plan.

Before the bus arrived with David's work crew, he explained his plan and discussed an additional porch problem with Coach. As they talked, David took more measurements on a two-by-four that he would cut into a baluster pattern for the crew. Minutes later his crew walked up the driveway, shook hands with Coach, and got their assignments.

David pulled the young men to the side for a review of the plan and assigned individuals to specific tasks. These young men also found their folders, wrote the step-by-step process of the day's assignment, put on their tool belts, and began work.

Fifteen minutes later, Coach stopped to check on the progress of David's plan and crew. Together they discussed the challenges of individual students. Coach worked one on one with each student before he moved inside the house to check on the closet and trim crews. Coach checked back with David or individuals on David's crew three more times during the afternoon session. By the end of the session, the porch railing had been reinstalled to the state and county construction code.

All students cleaned their work areas, put the tools into the tool trailer, and met with Coach for a brief conversation to name a skill or challenge they had managed effectively or set a goal for tomorrow's work as they shook hands with him.

Apply the Authenticity Test

Let's apply the authenticity test (see Figure 2.2) to David's English classroom and construction trades onsite classroom:

1. Is this practice or strategy something that an adult, experienced, literate person really does in the world outside of school?
2. Do the students understand its authenticity?

Figure 2.2. Application of the authenticity test.

Assignment	Used Outside of School	How and Why Used by Experienced Adults
English. Read a novel and answer questions in a study guide after reading each chapter.	**No.** At the heart of the lesson, the teacher is encouraging students to become engaged in reading this novel so that they want to continue reading other novels. However, the work students do is a school-based task making students accountable by answering questions.	This lesson suggests that adult readers move from novel to novel getting engaged in a next novel that is similar to the current one. However, readers who engage in book clubs do not complete study guides. Instead they join a community of readers to discuss and explore their personal understandings and interests.
Construction Trades. Assess construction of a porch railing that is out of code. Plan and repair the railing to meet county and state codes.	**Yes.** Students do the work of experienced adults in the field. They make a product for a client and work with the knowledge of county and state codes as a guide for quality and accountability.	This activity portrays the collaborative work environment that a construction tradesperson might encounter on any house construction job site. Students engage in the same tasks and expectation of quality decisions and craftsmanship that are embedded in the task.

What Can a Classroom Teacher Learn from Construction Trades?

If you are an English teacher or a teacher in a discipline or field other than construction trades, you may be wondering how this story connects to your curriculum and instruction. In an English classroom, students may not be so actively or so clearly engaged in disciplinary work in the same way as the students in the Construction Trades program. In that program, as students literally construct a home, they generate new knowledge and expertise in each daily task. Most disciplines are required to teach a curriculum filled with a great deal of content. However, we want to suggest that teachers in an ELA or other content area classroom, committed to engaging students in disciplinary work, can enact parallel authentic skills, habits, and strategies in some units of study or some tasks within a unit.

Observing the construction trades classroom side by side with English, science, social studies, and mathematics classrooms engaged in project-based and authentic learning experiences, we came to believe that students can appropriately do some tasks that fall in the category of "doing school." However, learning experiences in which students *just* "do school" can have a negative impact on student learning and identities. To make more sense of this idea, we developed a continuum, detailed in the next section, that describes characteristics of learning experiences that move from "doing school" to "doing authentic work" at the edge of a discipline or applied field of study.

Continuum of Disciplinary Literacy Learning: Doing Authentic Work

Across our educational careers, we have been drawn to creating and studying authentic disciplinary classrooms, contexts, and tasks. As we observed and studied various teachers, their classrooms, and their students, the definition of *authentic* became concrete but the images of these classrooms varied. There does not seem to be a single model for authentic disciplinary work, which is why we began researching authentic learning, disciplinary literacies, project-based learning, and the Maker Movement, as well as the development of identities, expertise, and agency.

NCTE's *Literacies* of *Disciplines* research brief calls us to teach for independent expertise: the ability to solve problems and be decision-makers applying the disciplinary specific knowledge and habits of experts in a field of study. Quality teaching and learning of this type already occurs in project-based learning (PBL) classrooms, Maker Movement events, after-school clubs, and classrooms of teachers working at and beyond the edges of traditional instruction and curricula.

As a result of what we've learned from this document and our own research, we returned to classrooms focused on complex disciplinary problems and authentic tasks, and we returned as well to the research on standards for authentic learning and pedagogy by Newmann and colleagues (1993, 1995), whom we mentioned in Chapter 1. We also read the work of Reeves, Herrington, and Oliver (2002), who define ten characteristics of authentic learning activities in online environments, and of Mehlinger (1995), who focuses on the impact of authentic learning in online environments on motivation. We explored the problem-based learning (PBL) going on at the Buck Institute for Education (BIE) and Nichole Pinkard's work with the Digital Youth Network. As we read this fascinating work, we began to compare the characteristics in each in order to create a mental map or framework to understand and name what we were observing in classrooms and hearing as teachers described the teaching and learning events in their classrooms.

Eventually, we synthesized the characteristics identified by multiple researchers and developed a continuum that graphically illustrates the range of learning experiences students might encounter across a unit or a year in a single teacher's classroom (see Figure 2.3). As you look through this continuum, imagine an English, science, or social studies classroom in which students create a written product typical of experts in that discipline. As the teacher designs the learning tasks, some tasks may appear more *foundational*, what we think of as "Learning for Use." These tasks develop prior knowledge, habits, and processes for students to use as they engage in authentic decision making as writers. These foundational lessons and tasks may be considered transitional as students and teachers alike move from doing school tasks that are predominately controlled and managed by the teacher to an independent decision-making model. This shift changes the thinking and instructional goal(s) from "right answers" and "right meanings" to multiple answers and multiple meanings. The teacher's role shifts from evaluator to modeler and mentor as students try on the habits, processes, and strategies. In other words, the work becomes more about the writer than the writing (Calkins, Hartman, & White, 2005). As students and teachers make this transition, students may identify and analyze evidence in a text to support an answer or explain how a technique or process enabled effective reading, writing, or thinking. Substantive conversations and higher-order thinking expected from foundational tasks also increase the level of engagement for students.

Moving to the middle column of the continuum in Figure 2.3, we suggest that some learning tasks may be *project-based*—that is, "Learning for Application and Decision Making within a School." For these tasks, students use foundational or prior knowledge, habits, processes, and strategies to engage in a project that extends across multiple days or weeks. Students may be developing new skills and processes in this work, but they will also be recalling expertise learned previously and generating new knowledge that extends their understanding of writing and writing decisions. Students encounter and imagine multiple solutions and manage

Figure 2.3. Continuum of disciplinary literacy learning: Doing authentic work. (Sources: This continuum is a synthesis of characteristics of authentic learning based on the work of Newmann, Secada, & Wehlage, 1995; Mehlinger, 1995; Reeves, Herrington, & Oliver, 2002; Buck Institute for Education, n.d.; Digital Youth Network, n.d.)

	Doing School Reproduction of Knowledge	**Doing the Discipline** Construction of Knowledge		
	Isolated/Episodic Learning *Learning for a Grade*	**Foundational Learning** *Learning for Use*	**Project-Based Learning** *Learning for Application and Decision Making within School*	**Authentic Learning** *Learning to Create for an Audience Beyond School*
Product or Performance	**SCHOOL TASK** 1. Identify elements, information, or processes in products and performances produced by others. 2. Express learning through brief responses: • True and false • Multiple choice • Fill-in-the-blank • Short sentences or responses (Newman, Secada, & Wehlage, 1995)	**REPLICATION TASK** 1. Use a step-by-step process outlined by the teacher or in imitation of performances produced by others. 2. Express learning through elaborated responses: • Include details and elaborations. • Expressed in brief and extended narratives, expositions, and arguments.	**CONSTRUCTED PRODUCT OR PERFORMANCE** 1. Analyze a proposed problem with multiple solutions to identify a plan and processes to create a product that addresses the problem. 2. Express learning through elaborated responses: • Include details, elaborations, and nuances. • Expressed in brief and extended narratives, expositions, and arguments. • Extended across time.	**CONSTRUCTED PRODUCT OR PERFORMANCE** 1. Design, innovate, or renovate a product or performance while examining competing solutions for multiple audiences beyond school. 2. Express learning through elaborated responses: • Represented in multiple ways. • Supported with details, elaborations, and nuances. • Expressed in short or extended narratives, expositions, and arguments. • Extended across time.
Individual or Collaborative Performance	**INDIVIDUAL** 3. Task generally completed alone.	**COLLABORATIVE** 3. Task completion requires peer interaction to learn or extend knowledge, process, product, or performance.	**COLLABORATIVE** 3. Task completion requires student choice and voice and peer interaction to manage resources, plan, adjust, and assess process, product, or performance. (BIE)	**COLLABORATIVE** 3. Task completion requires peer and expert interaction to problematize, adjust, systematize, and assess process, product, or performance.
Knowledge Development	**ACQUIRING CONTENT** 4. Accept prior knowledge as authoritative. 5. Survey information to memorize facts, label parts, distinguish types, and recognize similarity and difference. 6. Use teacher critique to evaluate acquisition of content.	**SENSE MAKING** 4. View knowledge as base for future work. 5. Organize, analyze, and synthesize information. 6. Use teacher or peer critique to define essential knowledge.	**KNOWLEDGE MAKING** 4. View knowledge from multiple perspectives. 5. Engage in inquiry to analyze, synthesize, and evaluate information, processes, genres, and/or reasoning. 6. Use teacher or peer critique to focus or extend knowledge.	**KNOWLEDGE MAKING** 4. View knowledge from multiple, competing perspectives. 5. Engage in inquiry to analyze, synthesize, and evaluate information, processes, and/or reasoning. 6. Use teacher or peer critique to identify and analyze complex ideas or create new thinking.

Continued on next page

Figure 2.3. Continued

	Doing School Reproduction of Knowledge	Doing the Discipline Construction of Knowledge		
	Isolated/Episodic Learning *Learning for a Grade*	Foundational Learning *Learning for Use*	Project-Based Learning *Learning for Application and Decision Making within School*	Authentic Learning *Learning to Create for an Audience Beyond School*
Expertise Development	**DEVELOP A SKILL TO COMPLETE A TASK** 7. Learn academic task, product, and/or process to become effective when doing school tasks. 8. Enact role of student to demonstrate grasp of content and concepts. 9. Apply expertise to become effective in next related school task or process. (Newmann, Secada, & Wehlage, 1995)	**DEVELOP EXPERTISE IN DEFINED TASK** 7. Learn foundational knowledge, skills, strategies, habits, tools, and processes of the discipline. 8. Enact and experiment with roles, skills, habits, and/or strategies to create knowledge that transfers to disciplinary tasks. 9. Reflect on expertise and work individually and within the group—i.e., peer and self-assessment. (Reeves, Herrington, & Oliver, 2002)	**APPLY EXPERTISE IN NEW TASK** 7. Retrieve foundational learning as expertise and apply to a new task. 8. Enact project-based roles to create knowledge that transfers to new tasks. 9. Reflect on expertise and work individually and within the group—i.e., peer and self-assessment. (Reeves, Herrington, & Oliver, 2002)	**APPLY EXPERTISE IN NEW TASK AND DISCIPLINE** 7. Retrieve and apply foundational learning as expertise while learning at the edge of the discipline. Routinely engage in imaginative and innovative activities. (Digital Youth Network, n.d.) 8. Enact role of expert to look for, test, and create relationships, patterns, and transfer knowledge within and across disciplines. (Newmann, Secada, & Wehlage, 1995) 9. Reflect on expertise and work individually and within the group to create and transfer knowledge to other disciplines. (Newmann, Secada, & Wehlage, 1995)
Role of Teacher	**TEACHER** 10. Demonstrate, assign, evaluate, or correct performance. 11. Evaluate and document success in school tasks. 12. Create value for academic achievement.	**COACH** 10. Model and coach performance, serving as a critical listener. 11. Assess and document competence in use of disciplinary knowledge, processes, and foundational tasks. Enable student self-assessment. 12. Create value beyond being a success in school. (Newmann, Secada, & Wehlage, 1995)	**COACH** 10. Model and coach performance, serving as a co-problem solver. 11. Collaboratively assess and document competence in application of disciplinary knowledge in complex tasks. 12. Create experience of and value for ideas, processes, and concepts in a discipline or applied field.	**THINKING PARTNER** 10. Serve as thinking partner and activator of student thinking. 11. Collaboratively assess and document achievement of personal and external standards. 12. Create experience of and value for a product or performance to impact the lives of others.

multiple resources as they research or study and write in various ways. In project-based learning, the teacher becomes a coach, co-expert, and sometimes co-learner. The learning focuses on a collaborative inquiry or a product designed and developed under the control of the student(s), who is meeting a standard for an audience beyond the teacher and possibly beyond the classroom.

Finally, as the third column represents, some learning tasks may require significant collaboration or development of authentic processes as students engage in *authentic experiences*, what we call "Learning to Create for an Audience beyond School." This kind of learning mirrors the tasks of writers, historians, scientists, and/or researchers. In authentic learning experiences, the teacher is both a coach and a thinking partner, providing regular feedback and recognizing the growing expertise of each student. This role also changes the students' position and responsibility. They are generating knowledge and products that have value and use beyond school in authentic work settings and for authentic audiences. This work may cause them to consider competing solutions and determine an effective approach from many possible approaches. Students have the opportunity to develop expertise through problem solving that demands recall and use of habits, processes, and strategies previously learned and most similar to the habits, processes, and strategies used by writers, historians, scientists, and/or researchers.

Applying the Continuum of Disciplinary Literacy Learning

The continuum has helped us unpack the complex teaching and learning that we have observed in classrooms that are moving toward authentic work in small and significant ways. It calls us to examine what students are doing and making and how disciplinary literacies enable that doing and making, and as well as how the environment and tasks develop student agency and independence. Let's apply the continuum to David's English and construction trades classrooms (see Figure 2.4).

This comparison provides more detail about the differences between David's two classroom encounters during one school day. It also illustrates that interactions in authentic disciplinary-based social settings can create a powerful identity, and that identity development can shift an individual's beliefs about himself and the world, which in turn can influence conscious actions (Moje, 2008). Onsite, David was self-initiating; he engaged in conversations with the instructor and other students to focus on a task that required problem solving, recall of prior knowledge, and generation of new knowledge through construction of a product intended for a client and assessed by adherence to state and county construction codes. Those powerful actions seem to suggest that developing a strong identity onsite transferred in specific ways to a traditional English classroom.

Figure 2.4. Comparison of David's English classroom and his construction trades onsite classroom.

	English Classroom	**Construction Trades Onsite**
Product or Performance	Students displayed school-congruent work habits to read and answer questions in a study guide.	Students used disciplinary work habits to collaboratively construct a porch as a team.
Individual or Collaborative Performance	Students worked alone.	Peers engaged in substantive conversations with team leader and coworkers as well as the teacher to recall processes, to solve a problem, and to apply knowledge of state and county codes to construct and evaluate the performance.
Knowledge Development	Students listened as the teacher and several students demonstrated use of context to define vocabulary.	Students applied prior knowledge of framing and pattern making as they developed new knowledge of state and county codes for porch construction.
Expertise Development	Students used classroom-specific behaviors to complete a routine academic task.	Students developed and applied discipline-specific strategies, decision making, and language to interact and solve a complex problem. In brief conversations, they used peer and self-assessment to evaluate and maintain the quality of their work.
Role of Teacher	The teacher provided support for volunteers who demonstrated using context to define words. And the teacher expressed personal value for reading and appreciation for science fiction.	The teacher served as thinking partner to David as he prepared for his role as team leader. He also served as coach in routine teacher and student conversations during construction of porch and closet trim.

Working every afternoon in a disciplinary work environment, David had adopted the identity of a construction trades craftsperson. He realized that errors and problem solving are inherent in construction and understood the necessity for precise work. This combination developed his commitment to quality workmanship. In addition, he valued being part of a team and gained essential skills as a team leader.

In a follow-up interview, David explained that his commitment to quality work onsite had become a habit that enabled him to self-monitor during English. He did not always know how to do school work successfully. In previous years, David would have been the student sleeping, texting, or drawing a video game character on his notebook. Now he realized that he had to do what it took in school to graduate so he could go to college for construction management. David claimed that he learned how to do school by building homes on sunny days and in the midst of snowstorms, making mistakes and repairing them, talking through his thinking with Coach Moscovic and team members, and reading and writing in his construction notebook. In the construction work, David gained a vision of himself as confident and competent, which helped him to focus in school settings.

Authentic Disciplinary Work: Designing a Program

As we studied Dick Moscovic and Duane Olds's Construction Trades Two-Year Program, it became clear that they have implemented activities and tasks across the continuum of disciplinary literacy learning; while some we recognize as *doing school*, most fall in the three stages of *doing the discipline*. Duane, who primarily teaches the first year of the two-year program, explains:

> When they arrive, students are used to desks and paper–and-pencil tasks. Even if they hate them and want to escape them, they have difficulty moving to tasks they have no experience with. To do hands-on work, students need to develop confidence and a belief that they can make something. At first students are skeptical of their ability to use the tools. Saws, routers, ladders, and scaffolding frighten them. Eventually, they realize they can make something; and the more they do the work, the more they believe that they are competent and skilled.
>
> To gain confidence, they make mistakes. See all the siding trim on the floor? That is learning. It takes time to get the measuring and sequence of a job right. They have to develop a sense of how things go together and understand a whole process. And it takes some paper-and-pencil work, but most of the work has to be hands-on.
>
> As students gain knowledge and expertise, they teach each other techniques— simple tasks like applying mastic to lay ceramic tile or more complex tasks like using a square to create a stringer for a staircase. They transfer knowledge gained doing projects in the shop to real-world work onsite. For example, they learn how to roof a dollhouse standing on the shop floor; then they use that knowledge to solve the problems that emerge on a real house. But now they are doing the task ten feet off the ground and standing on a 5/12 pitch roof.

On one visit to Duane's shop, we talked with a young woman who was roofing a dollhouse. Duane introduced Kierra to us, explaining that she and Brittany took third place in the Holiday Invitational Masonry Competition. We asked her why she decided to take construction trades. Kierra explained:

> I wanted to do hands-on learning. It is easier to learn hands-on because [the teachers] don't just show you. Instead of taking notes, doing worksheets, and taking tests, you actually try what you are learning. I learned to mix mortar and lay brick in the fall, and then used those trowel skills to pour and finish a concrete driveway. I also used what I've learned to work with my father doing construction jobs.

Continuum of Key Instructional Tasks in the Construction Trades Two-Year Program

The continuum in Figure 2.5 provides a sampling of the tasks and projects across the continuum that students experience in the Construction Trades Two-Year Program. This demonstrates that students experience a full range of tasks or

Figure 2.5. Continuum of key instructional tasks in the Construction Trades Two-Year Program.

Doing School Reproduction of Knowledge	Doing the Discipline Construction of Knowledge		
Isolated/Episodic Learning	Foundational Learning	Project-Based Learning	Authentic Learning
Learning for a Grade	*Learning for Use*	*Learning for Application and Decision Making within School*	*Learning to Create for an Audience beyond School*
SHORT-TERM TASKS • Exercises in carpentry math book	**SHORT-TERM TASKS** • Machine tool exercise • Safety certification • Tools certification • Construction notebooks • Blueprint reading • Materials ordering • Professional etiquette	**LONG-TERM PROJECTS** • Anatomy of a home • Block and brick masonry corner • Platform shed • Mock house framing and wiring • Drywall: hanging and finishing • Interior trim: doors and windows • Staircase construction • Exterior siding and trim: fabrication and installation	**LONG-TERM PROJECTS** • Wheelchair ramp for Christmas in April • Playhouse for SCAMP charity auction • New home construction for Lighthouse • Nature center bunkhouse construction for city of Auburn Hills • Renovation of homes for Grace Centers of Hope substance abuse center
COMPUTER-BASED LEARNING ***ACT Key Train*** • Mathematics • Reading for information • Locating information	**COMPUTER-BASED LEARNING** • Applied mathematics in professional work habits • Occupational Safety and Health Administration (OSHA): National industry safety certification	**COMPETITIONS** • Novice Carpentry Invitational • Holiday Carpentry and Masonry Invitational	**COMPETITIONS** • Skills USA: local, regional, state, national

projects that move toward the capstone project of building or remodeling a house. This continuum shows the range of activities in a two-year program that is focused on authentic achievement. In this program, you might expect that all of the activities would be authentic. But that is not the case. Certainly the majority of activities fall in the Doing the Discipline columns, but many activities are foundational.

If you look at column four, you will notice that all projects have an authentic client beyond school. Most of the clients are nonprofit organizations. Dick and Duane are constantly searching for the next nonprofit partnership to maintain an authentic onsite experience for all students.

It is important to note here that not all construction trades programs create products for clients. Many programs are textbook or computer based. Students spend most of their time in classrooms and only some of their time in a shop building a wall or framing a partial house that the students tear down at the end of the year. In those classrooms, authentic experience is lost. A client never arrives onsite and asks for a change or compliments the work with excitement and admiration for the young people who built it. A county inspector never stops to evaluate the work and put a green (approved) or a red (stop work) tag on the front window of the building. In contrast, when students learn in authentic contexts, the tools, language, actions, and structures in use help develop critical thinking in a discipline and across fields that exist in the real world.

Duane Olds may be like many teachers who design an end-in-mind curriculum that provides students with a mix of foundational and authentic learning experiences. Central to maintaining an authentic context balanced with foundational learning, Duane identifies new real-world clients and projects each year. Each activity or project provides opportunities for students to form habits and skills as well as to construct new learning and apply prior learning. As we watched the work unfold across a year, we discovered that some experiences were carefully designed for foundational and project-based work in the shop. But many experiences grew out of a range of nonprofit partnerships. These authentic experiences allowed students to transfer knowledge from foundational exercises and to construct new knowledge or learn new skills engaging in work for clients.

The variety of exercises and projects demonstrates how habits, processes, and knowledge of tools and codes are examples of learning in one activity that then transfers to the next task, and then the next, across the year. You can track the conscious design of Dick and Duane's curriculum and experiences in Figure 2.6. In September, students completed the machine tool exercise to gain experience with the concept of self-monitoring accuracy while learning how to use basic tools. The ten tools used to complete this task were then used in multiple projects across the year. In November, students built a staircase in the shop. This project provided more complex experience with routers, which were used in the machine tool exercise in September. On this project, students used several different routers on the handrail, balusters, and treads of the staircase. In April and May, students used many of the same tools from the tool exercise to frame, roof, and trim the playhouse for a charity auction.

Clearly, Duane has designed a classroom for authentic learning experiences. So what can a teacher do who wants these same kinds of experiences but who has a classroom with thirty desks? Laura Mahler has a great deal to say about designing authentic learning experiences for her students in Advanced Placement Literature (AP Lit). She knows that the typical AP Lit course focuses primarily on reading literature and writing explication and argumentative essays. However, she has inserted several short units in which students take on the role of writer to create their own texts using the habits, strategies, and processes of the writers they are studying. We asked her to review the continuum of disciplinary literacy learning and reflect on how she applies the continuum to her instruction, her units across the year, and her students' learning.

Figure 2.6. Examples of year 1 learning across the continuum of key instructional tasks.

Foundational Learning	Project-Based Learning	Authentic Learning
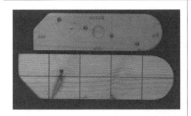		
September—Machine Tool Exercise Students complete this tool exercise after they achieve tool safety certification. The exercise requires accuracy with a wide range of tools that will eventually be used in construction projects.	**December—Stair Construction Project** In the shop, teams of students develop knowledge of codes and expertise with tools for staircase and railing construction.	**October—Bunkhouse Foundation** Students pour the foundation for a bunkhouse at Hawk Woods Nature Center. Next students install the slab and lay the block for the foundation of the bunkhouse that was built by year 2 students.
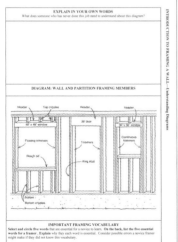		
November—Basics of Framing Students develop disciplinary language in this paper-and-pencil task.	**February—Masonry Competition** Students are given blueprints and sufficient materials to complete a project in 5 hours. They also take a test on content knowledge. Eventually, Ryan won first place in Michigan's SkillsUSA Masonry Competition in 2012.	**April—Charity Auction** A team of students built this playhouse for a local charity. The playhouse is a replica of a historic home in Clarkson, Michigan. The students built the house from architectural blueprints created by local architect Robyn Johnston.

How Does an Advanced Placement English Teacher Do Authentic Disciplinary Work?

Laura Mahler
English Department, Clarkston High School

Partnerships: Clarkson High School English Department; Regional Network: Oakland Writing Project (OWP); National Network: National Writing Project (NWP) and Literacy Design Collaborative (LDC).

Laura Mahler, who teaches Advanced Placement Literature at Clarkston High School, also sees her instruction as operating in all areas of the continuum of disciplinary literacy learning. Unlike many AP Lit teachers, Laura inserts eight weeks of authentic writing into her yearlong course that prepares students for the AP Lit test. During those eight weeks, students identify a genre for deep study and write fiction, poetry, memoirs, essays, or a screenplay for publication. The work is divided into a three-cycle workshop integrated across the first two trimesters of the course.

Writing Cycle I occurs in early fall. In this three-week unit, students establish a writer's notebook and a writing life. As Laura describes it, they live wide-awake to their world in and out of the classroom to discover and explore ideas and stories in their daily lives. She provides brief but explicit lessons on generating ideas and making universal decisions in craft and structure that are used across genres. Students also read and experiment with multiple genres and eventually select a single genre for self-study. Student writing throughout this writing cycle is exploratory and experimental. Much of the writing supports deeper study and may be abandoned in later writing cycles. Students establish writer response groups in which they share their early entries and receive feedback from fellow writers, who notice and wonder about the texts as well as suggest opportunities embedded in the entries for related entries or drafting.

Writing Cycle II occurs midyear. In this two-week unit, students develop a self-study of annotating the decisions of several writers across a single genre to develop a repertoire of devices and structures. Then students use this repertoire of decisions in their own writing. They develop early drafts of texts by rereading and selecting ideas and entries that emerged in Cycle I. They may also take a draft through revisions, moving it closer to a finished product. Students read calls for submission and imagine goals for publication. Writer response groups continue to support peers as they share and develop thoughtfully crafted writing for a larger audience.

Writing Cycle III occurs in early spring. In this three-week unit, students review, identify, and select specific calls for submission and publication. The work shifts to the development of a portfolio and formatting of finished work for submission. Students engage in brief lessons, conferences with Laura and peers, as well as response groups to consider and write for an audience beyond school.

Laura arranges her lessons and time usage to create a workshop environment that allows students to engage with foundational learning in order to replicate the lives of writers, but she also extends the work with independent choices and decision making. This positions her students as writers with writing lives in which they can enact the disciplinary knowledge they are gaining both in the workshop cycles and in the whole-class study of canonical texts. In each cycle, students write reflections and prepare for end-of-cycle exit interviews with Laura.

Figure 2.7 provides a brief look into one student's writer's notebook and portfolio across the three cycles. It demonstrates how the early work established foundational habits that focused Harrison's study in Cycle II and transferred to authoring decisions in Cycle III. The excerpt from a poem entry, "As the Bird Flies," changed across time as it emerged into a new poem, "The Veiled Cage." Harrison's reflection describes how the writers he chose to study and his response group work impacted the choices he made to revise an early poem entry from his writer's notebook:

> I originally began the poem one day when I was outside, and I thought about a few birds flying around. I finished the first draft and found there really wasn't much story to it, so I shoved some meaning into the same structure, and it ended up very incoherent. My goal in Cycle III was to radically revise the poem by finalizing my meaning first and then writing the poem to fit the meaning.
>
> Once the new poem was written, I continued [revising] through peer and teacher reviews [as well as] posting it online. . . . I learned, despite my best intentions, there were parts of the poem too obscure for most readers to understand. My diction and sentence structure was confusing. I needed to switch some of that.

We asked Laura: why have students do three writing cycles that require significant project-based and authentic work in order to write for publication when you are also preparing them for a rigorous Advanced Placement test? Laura explained:

> I know that time is precious to the AP Literature teacher. There seems to be so much to teach in the relatively short span of a school year to adequately prepare students for the demands of the AP Literature test and for the demands of college writing.

Figure 2.7. Excerpts from Harrison's writing across Cycles I, II, and III.

Project-Based Learning Early Fall—Cycle I	Project-Based Learning Midyear—Cycle II	Early Spring—Cycle III
Develop a writing life by living wide-awake. Read the world to find ideas. Establish and generate work in a writer's notebook. Read widely in the genre.	Read and study the devices and structures of a range of writers and a single author. Develop theories about how and why writers use a repertoire of devices and structures. Generate and revise based on study and mentoring activities.	Review calls for submission. Identify texts for submission from a portfolio of work. Revise, edit, and format texts for submission.
Poem Entry	**Bibliography of Annotated Works**	**Opening of Final Poem Draft**
"As the Bird Flies"	**Short Stories**	"The Veiled Cage"
As the bird flies, the follower, with no wings to beat, or heart to flutter, takes the wind for his own.	Mary Gordon, "Separation" Elizabeth Graver, "The Body Shop" Salman Rushdie, "Good Advice Is Rarer Than Rubies" and "Chekhov and Zulu"	Two winged creatures take to the air. Far away across land and warm currents that sweep them along and Together.
Wings beat and stir the air, colors swirl and shift behind, as she runs with him, and she feels free.	**Genre Study—Poetry** Billy Collins, *Introduction to Poetry* Jane Shore, *Music Minus One* Edward Brathwaite, "Chad" Edwin Brock, "Evolution" Edgar Allan Poe, "The Raven" Gary Soto, "Mission Tire Factory, 1969" Walt Whitman, "O Captain My Captain"	Together they fly, their wings beat and stir the sky. Colors swirl behind in patterns of Freedom.
The follower, like water, flows on the current, And with the wind. He runs with her, and he is free.		Freedom to fly, to be alive and to give a gift to those who give themselves, but receive only pain, outside, inside. A gift of Love.

However, in order for students to see a clear connection between the reciprocal skills of reading and writing, it is well worth the time invested to have them creating their own writing products for publication as well as writing the literary essays that they will see on the AP test and in college classrooms.

In my class, students write throughout the first semester in three writing cycles. Each cycle has a general aim and establishes what I think of as a layer of a writing life and writing habits.

Using three cycles spaced apart over time allows the writing time to *cool* so that students return to the writing with fresh eyes and a more objective view of what they wrote a few weeks ago. Students participate in writer response groups in each cycle, which allows them to see what sense another reader makes of their writing. It allows the writer to step outside of him- or herself to see the writing as others do. This allows a view of conceptions and confusions that the writer usually doesn't see when working alone.

Overall, students emerge far more aware of the impact [that] writers' decisions [have] on meaning. They are better prepared to look for alternatives that a writer could have chosen and, therefore, to come to conclusions about why the writer chose to make the decision that she or he did make. Their understanding of poetry, essay, and story is so much deeper because of this work. And this knowledge transfers to reading, analyzing, and writing about the fiction and poetry they encounter for the first time on the AP test.

Figure 2.8 provides a sampling of tasks that Laura's students encounter in the three authentic writing cycles compared to a sampling of tasks from the literature, literary essays, and criticism students read, as well as the literary explications and essays students write. She imagines that Cycle I and Cycle II would be called project-based work since students write for themselves and the class. However, Cycle III moves students to consider a wider audience than that of teacher and peers as they revisit work that might have been finished in an earlier cycle for submission to magazines and writing competitions. Laura also includes a few key tasks that might be considered doing school and a single unit on American drama. This continuum does not include all the units and tasks that engage her students in reading literature, critical reviews, and essays and in writing academic essays for college readiness and AP test preparation.

How Can a Teacher Move toward "Doing the Discipline"?

Possibly the first step teachers might take in moving toward doing the discipline is giving themselves permission to move slowly using the authenticity test and the continuum of disciplinary literacy learning as guides.

Some teachers may start by changing a single task or product in a unit. As Figure 2.9 indicates, the task or product that students perform or create determines the characteristics of the learning experience. Teachers might design tasks that encourage any of the following: student choice, peer interaction and collaboration, or enactment of a role requiring disciplinary expertise to complete. Each of these characteristics shifts the position of the student in the learning experience and provides the student with an opportunity to independently construct and use knowledge, make decisions, and/or manage multiple perspectives.

Some teachers start by shifting their own role or position in the learning experience. Instead of being the primary authority and critic of student work, they shift to modeling, becoming a critical listener, and coaching students. Or they insert moments for students to self-assess and reflect on their current work, their growth across time, their ability to use the tools of disciplinary experts, and their ability to set goals for future work or learning experiences.

Figure 2.8. Continuum of key instructional tasks: Writing and publishing cycles and academic writing.

Doing School Reproduction of Knowledge	Doing the Discipline Construction of Knowledge		
Isolated/Episodic Learning *Learning for a Grade*	**Foundational Learning** *Learning for Use*	**Project-Based Learning** *Learning for Application and Decision Making within School*	**Authentic Learning** *Learning to Create for an Audience beyond School*
SHORT-TERM TASKS Advanced Placement Test Preparation ■ Academic essay and AP test essay formats and structures ■ AP test multiple-choice question analysis ■ Integrated grammar activities	**SHORT-TERM TASKS Advanced Placement Analysis and Interpretation** ■ Study the impact of audience on authoring decisions. ■ Close rereading of a genre: structure, craft, purpose. ■ Analyze four essays by Arthur Miller about *Death of a Salesman* to analyze the intentions of the play and the techniques Miller uses to portray those intentions. ■ Analyze literary criticism of Miller and his works. ■ Analyze key elements in a scene as well as reimagine the scene's intent when creating a contemporary perspective. ■ Reread to identify revision decisions on an essay.	**LONG-TERM PROJECTS Writing Cycle I—3 weeks** ■ Create a writer's notebook and a writing life—habits and process for generating and revising writing. ■ Collect texts to compile a personal anthology. ■ Write exercises and invitations to apprentice craft, structure, and genre-based decisions of writers. ■ Attend a writer response group (2–3 times). **Writing Cycle II—2 weeks** ■ Reread notebook entries. ■ Identify appropriate audience(s) for writing in notebook. ■ Identify drafts or generate new work for submission to class book. ■ Read, study, and annotate a range of authors in a genre of choice. ■ Mentor syntactical and grammatical decisions of writers. ■ Attend writer response group (2 times).	**LONG-TERM PROJECTS Writing Cycle III—3 weeks** ■ Review portfolio of writing to develop and self-manage a body of work for publication beyond school. ■ Review calls for submissions and gather submission guidelines. ■ Manage a generation and/or revision process for publication beyond school. ■ Attend writer response group (2–3 times). ■ Format text according to submission guidelines and submit for publication.
Submit to be graded by teacher ■ Creation of products graded by teacher ■ Released AP essays	**Submit to be graded by teacher with student reflection and self-assessment** ■ Annotated close reading(s) ■ Reader's notebook and reading logs ■ Analysis and explication writing ■ Literary analysis essay	**Submit to be graded through collaborative (teacher and student) assessment and growth over time** ■ Submit to juried class or school publication(s). ■ Create digital products to be shared within classroom.	**Submit for use by audience beyond school** ■ Submit to calls for publication. ■ Submit to local, state, and national competitions. ■ Create digital products accessible online: wiki, etc.

Figure 2.9. Impact of task on student learning.

	Doing School Reproduction of Knowledge	Doing the Discipline Construction of Knowledge		
	Isolated/Episodic Learning *Learning for a Grade*	Foundational Learning *Learning for Use*	Project-Based Learning *Learning for Application and Decision Making within School*	Authentic Learning *Learning to Create for an Audience beyond School*
Assignment and Product	Read *Frankenstein* and take notes during class discussions and lectures. Write an essay from the following prompt: How does Shelley portray Victor? What is the true cause of his suffering?	After reading *Frankenstein*, collaboratively read several critical reviews of the novel and essays about Shelley's life. Identify an idea for an essay. Plan, draft, revise, and edit the essay based on peer feedback.	After reading *Frankenstein*, collaboratively analyze the novel's relevance to contemporary teen readers. Create a contemporized dramatization of a key scene and its thematic issue(s).	After reading *Frankenstein*, design and organize a symposium on bioethics for a community audience.
Key Characteristics	• Identifies elements or information produced by others • Accomplished alone • Accepts prior knowledge as authoritative • Uses teacher critique to identify acquisition of content • Learns academic task • Demonstrates grasp of content or concepts	• Uses step-by-step process in elaborated response • Requires peer interaction • Organizes, analyzes, and synthesizes information • Bases decisions on choice and self-interest • Uses teacher or peer critique • Learns processes of the discipline	• Analyzes a problem to create a product that addresses the problem expressed through an elaborated response • Requires peer interaction • Views knowledge from multiple perspectives • Uses teacher or peer critique • Enacts project-based roles	• Designs a performance for an audience beyond school extended across time • Requires peer and expert interaction • Views knowledge from multiple competing perspectives • Engages in inquiry • Enacts role of expert

Insights

As we observed a range of teachers attempting to engage students in disciplinary literacies, we realized that some contexts and building systems are more supportive than others. Implementing disciplinary literacies works better when a school agrees that authentic work is important and when teachers collaborate to put curriculum and instructional practices in place that support disciplinary learning. As we talked with teachers and students featured in this book, we had four insights:

1. Two learners engaged in the same authentic task may be operating or experiencing the task in different areas of the continuum.

2. Teachers may decrease the level of thinking in doing and making work when they break the task into small parts with a "correct" or predictable outcome or when they inadvertently reduce decision making so that there is little or no problem solving.

3. Not every task in a unit of study or unit in a curricular year will fall into the project-based or authentic categories of the continuum.

4. Moving from "doing school" to "doing the discipline" is a personal journey for each teacher. Finding a collaborative partner or team provides the creative and critical support.

As you engage in the Collegial Conversations at the end of each chapter, we suggest that you think about your own classroom lessons and units of study and the ways you might shift your instruction as well.

Collegial Conversations: How might you and your colleagues apply the continuum of disciplinary literacy learning?

Find a colleague with whom you can collaboratively apply the continuum of disciplinary literacy learning to an assignment and product (see Figure 2.10). Or identify a unit or a series of connected units that construct student knowledge and engage students in disciplinary literacies. Review the assignments, activities, tasks, projects, and products and place them in the continuum. As you fill in the continuum,

- Notice the types and range of learning in which students are already engaged.

- Imagine how you might adjust an activity or task to move it into another area of the continuum (see Figure 2.11).

Figure 2.10. Blank continuum for identifying the impact of a task on student learning.

	Doing School Reproduction of Knowledge	Doing the Discipline Construction of Knowledge		
	Isolated/Episodic Learning *Learning for a Grade*	Foundational Learning *Learning for Use*	Project-Based Learning *Learning for Application and Decision Making within School*	Authentic Learning *Learning to Create for an Audience beyond School*
Assignment and Product				
Key Characteristics				

Figure 2.11. Blank continuum for collaborative exploration of disciplinary literacies.

Doing School Reproduction of Knowledge	Doing the Discipline Construction of Knowledge		
Isolated/Episodic Learning *Learning for a Grade*	Foundational Learning *Learning for Use*	Project-Based Learning *Learning for Application and Decision Making within School*	Authentic Learning *Learning to Create for an Audience beyond School*
SHORT-TERM TASKS	SHORT-TERM TASKS	LONG-TERM PROJECTS	LONG-TERM PROJECTS
Submit to be graded by teacher	Submit to be graded by teacher with student reflection and self-assessment	Submit for collaborative assessment and growth over time	Submit for use by audience beyond school

Fronting Disciplinary Lenses

*A discipline is a more complex structure; to be engaged in a discipline is
to shape, and be shaped by, the subject, to be part of a scholarly community, to engage with fellow students—to become "disciplined."*
—Jan Parker, "A New Disciplinarity"

As we saw in the last chapter, creating contexts that support
authentic work is key in traveling down the road to authentic
literacies. A second important practice we learned from our work
and observations in schools is helping students learn to see tasks
through disciplinary lenses.

We would like to suggest that disciplines are communities of knowledge
making in which people share ways to "determin(e) ends and means, approaches and procedures, ways to judge disciplinary findings, the bases on which to
agree or disagree, and problems apprehended" (Christie & Maton, 2011, p. 5).
Disciplinary lenses, then, would be the tools and the intellectual framework
of a particular discipline or field. When teaching with attention to disciplinary
lenses, a teacher tends to highlight the habits of mind, introduce and revisit

the intellectual framework repeatedly, and have students use the tools of the discipline.

Disciplinarity is an important concept, even in a world sometimes claiming that disciplines are "dead," outmoded, or "elite forms of thought and education that exclude the experiences of many groups in society" (Christie & Maton, 2011, p. 3). The reason it is important is that although problems, ideas, and issues spill across disciplinary boundaries, the knowledge and tools encapsulated within a discipline such as mathematics or biology can provide angles of vision that often help address a problem or situation.

As a practicing teacher, you probably zeroed in on a discipline first in secondary school, when you named your favorite subject, and then again when you selected a major in college. You likely find the content interesting and the ways of working a pretty good fit for your strengths as a learner. But just because you've selected a discipline for your focus doesn't mean you have had opportunities to glimpse its knowledge-making edge, or to understand deeply the ways that various disciplines are constructed, or to see the applications of disciplinary knowledge in particular professions. And yet we're convinced that delving more deeply into our own chosen disciplines and the disciplines of our colleagues is important for revising professional practice to better serve our students. We need to "do our own disciplines" and then create circumstances in which students can learn to "do a discipline" with consciousness of that specific lens. "Doing" and "making" are just as key to understanding disciplinary lenses as they are to the kind of authentic work we talked about in the last chapter. For most students to understand why they would ever want to delve into a subject, they need to see groups of highly engaged people using knowledge to solve problems and making new knowledge in meaningful ways.

Attending to Disciplinary Lenses

How can we be sure that we have a good bead on the disciplines we're trying to introduce to students? We have identified five questions that can help practitioners try to ensure that they are moving toward using disciplinary lenses:

1. What **technical language** is used by adult practitioners in a discipline or field?

2. What **big questions** are asked by leaders and by learners in the discipline or field?

3. What **processes** are used **for making new knowledge or for sharing advances** in the discipline or field?

4. Where is the **"edge" of knowledge making** currently in the discipline or field?

5. What are the **habits of mind** we would see in a highly skilled practitioner of the discipline or field?

For instance, in a recent book, *Reading like a Historian: Teaching Literacy in Middle and High School History Classrooms* (2013), history education researchers Samuel Wineburg, Daisy Martin, and Chauncey Monte-Sano have gathered source documents, key questions, and possible activities about eight events in American history to provide a good starting point as social studies, government, and history teachers begin traveling a disciplinary road. As we studied their book and thought about the possible answers they might give to our five questions, we inferred they might respond with something like the material in Figure 3.1. If a teacher doesn't introduce multiple accounts of events, using primary and secondary documents, artifacts, and photographs, and if that teacher isn't having students engage in sourcing, corroborating, and argument making, then he or she has not yet begun to travel the road toward authentic disciplinary literacy.

The Problem of Language and Meaning

So what do we mean by engaging students in disciplinary lenses? Let's start by thinking about language and how language takes on specific meanings in specific subject areas. In math, English, history, music, fine arts, and science, we all use everyday words like *inquiry, problem solving, observation, reading,* and *writing,* but we mean significantly different things by these words. Our disciplinary lenses determine our meanings. But sometimes even we as teachers don't grasp how different these meanings truly are—which can lead to our students' confusion as they move across their school day. For example, *observation* in mathematics tends

Figure 3.1. Five questions to move toward disciplinary lenses—history example.

Technical Language	Primary source, secondary source, document, artifact, account, corroboration
Big Questions	Why is this historical event important enough to analyze and unpack? What does this event teach us about this period in history? About who we are currently, as people and citizens? For example, "Did Pocahontas rescue John Smith?" Or "What caused the Dust Bowl? What story gets told?" (Wineburg, Martin, & Monte-Sano, 2013, p. xi)
Processes	Interpreting or reinterpreting a historical event by seeking documentary evidence and interrogating texts; "piecing together fragments in an act of creation" (Wineburg, Martin, & Monte-Sano, 2013, p. x)
Knowledge-Making Edge	Produce a new, sourced narrative account of an event that leads to people viewing it differently. For example, *The Empire of Necessity: Slavery, Freedom, and Deception in the New World* (Greg Grandin, 2014)
Habits of Mind	Sourcing, questioning, contextualizing, considering multiple accounts, corroborating, managing multiple causes and paradox, making generalizations, systematically arguing

to be empirical, whereas *observation* in English class may include both sensory and emotional information. A mathematician or scientist observing a plant, for example, would measure the plant's height using a tool, describe it precisely, trace its genus in a notebook, and perhaps make a fairly exact scientific drawing or generate a cross-sectional diagram of the cut stem. A poet observing a plant might generate metaphors and include feelings and connections to other experiences, record them in a journal, and then sketch an impression. A historian might explore the evolutionary history of a plant or its life cycle through both observation and study of historical accounts, drawings, and photographs. If we teachers truly understand the differences between various kinds of observation, we are better able to clarify for students what we're undertaking in our discipline and what counts as "effective" in different contexts.

We have learned from civil rights organizer and Algebra Project founder Bob Moses that philosopher Willard Van Orman Quine said that mathematics and science use "regimented speech" (Harrison-Barbet, 2008). Quine, Bob's teacher, noted that everyday language was placed in a "straightjacket" in mathematics and science. But it is straightjacketed purposefully in order to make new kinds of knowledge. "Straightjacketing," in this case, is not necessarily negative; by putting limits on and parameters around language use, certain features that are key for mathematics and science knowledge making—concepts such as height and volume and directionality—are highlighted, which then makes deeper inquiry possible without the distraction of other features. Once Bob Moses understood how differently language was used in math and science, he began to develop ways for struggling students to learn how to move from one register to another—consciously and purposefully—so they could actually join the discourse community of mathematics with a sense of agency and purpose.

The Algebra Project, a national network involving practitioners, mathematics educators, and mathematicians aiming to transform math learning for struggling students, developed curricula built around a framework that begins with a common experience and then moves from *people talk*, the Algebra Project term for everyday speech, to *feature talk*—a kind of talk that highlights mathematically salient features such as "compared to" and "taller than." Curricular projects then engage students in generating *iconic representation(s)*, student-generated drawings that explain through their symbols what is happening, followed by a transition to *abstract symbolic representation*, the conventional mathematical way to represent problems. This act of helping students deliberately shift in a step-by-step process from everyday speech and phenomena to a formal mathematical representation is referred to as "mathematizing" (see Figure 3.2). For the Algebra Project, the foundation of a common, active experience is a beginning point that places students who have not been well served in schools on new ground. Teachers and students begin by using

Figure 3.2. Algebra Project mathematizing framework.

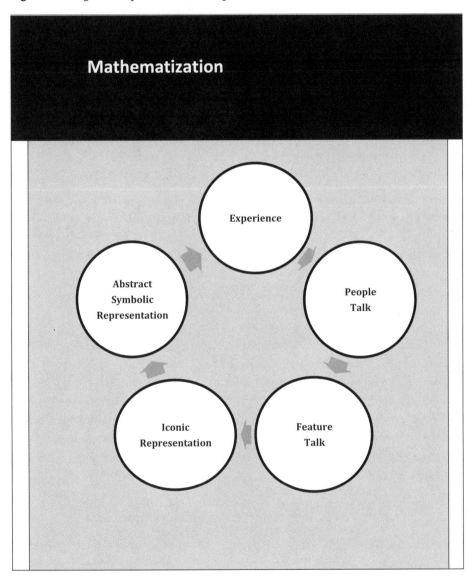

everyday language about phenomena, communicated through both talk and writing, identified as people talk:

> "If you start at the window, and move three and one-half steps to the left, you will arrive at the teacher's desk."

From there, students begin to work their way to important features of mathematical and scientific work, known as feature talk:

Figure 3.3. Iconic representation.

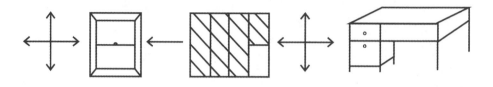

"The location of the window is three and one-half *units* to the left of the location of the teacher's desk."

Students then have an opportunity to draw, model, and label in an iconic manner that "makes sense" of the concept to them and their peers, the step of iconic representation (see Figure 3.3). Eventually, they transition to the mathematical symbol system used by people around the world, abstract symbolic representation:

$$x = -3\frac{1}{2} + y$$

By explicitly teaching the movement from everyday communication to formal mathematical communication, the Algebra Project makes it possible for students to participate in the disciplinary community they are now in and to grasp how language is used in that community. Bob and his Algebra Project colleagues have taught us that shifting from everyday speech to speech that has credibility within a discipline or field is not at all automatic and may require lots of practice and a clear bead on the difficulties involved in acquiring new language and grammars. If teachers rush to abstract symbolic representation, students may not be making sense of the mathematical concepts. This approach develops a way of reading and writing in mathematics.

What Can Other Disciplines Learn from This Framework?

What would it mean for teachers in other disciplines to try on this same framework, helping students to understand how language is used in their professional communities? In some parts of the country, teachers have attempted to do just that. In the Algebra Project, as in other experiential learning efforts, units and projects begin with carefully selected experiences that are then unpacked in order to build key content concepts and introduce important work practices. Student activities can then culminate in sharing knowledge or learning with audiences outside of the classroom. A good starting place for collaboration across disciplines might be Trip Line, a foundational Algebra Project unit that begins with a literal trip, followed by careful work on representing and mathematizing the trip, so that students ultimately can grasp and cement an understanding of the number line and how to envision and work with positive and negative integers.

A carefully designed field trip can launch Trip Line mathematical work while also launching work in social studies/history and language arts. Key concepts in English language arts include sequencing a narrative and the "line" of an argument. Key concepts in social studies/history include chronology and the understanding that historical perspectives are shaped by role, position, milieu, and historical moment. What if the organized trip raised issues of civil rights history and contemporary justice work, initiating various informational, argumentative, and aesthetic writings as well as raising important mathematical concepts such as subtraction as comparison, directionality, and the role of a number line? All along the way, teachers across disciplines could compare notes on student understandings and refer back to a common framework.

No individual teacher is likely to have a deep enough understanding of a wide range of disciplines and their requirements to be able to frame problems on his or her own. However, a team of teachers who have taken the time and trouble to deepen their disciplinary understandings can together design a project or frame a problem for their students so that youth have a chance to grasp the affordances and limitations of various disciplinary lenses.

The journey toward deeper disciplinarity and more authentic work is just that—a journey. There is no need to judge yourself harshly just because you are partway down a road. In the next two vignettes, we present two teachers who are at different points on the journey. It can be informative to look closely at such examples because they begin to illuminate next steps that can be taken to keep moving along.

An Illustration of the Power of Disciplinarity: Two Vignettes

In the following illustration, two middle school science teachers, Mr. Knott and Ms. Amari,[3] and their students are working with the same basic content—a unit entitled "What is the water like in our river?" Both teachers are actively engaged in improving their practice, but the second teacher, Ms. Amari, has gone further down the path toward authentic disciplinary work, providing students with more opportunities to learn what scientific inquiry and professional practice look and sound like.

Mr. Knott's Classroom

As his twenty-nine students enter the room, Mr. Knott, a well-respected, fifteen-year science teacher, begins class by telling students to get out their investigation sheets and check their bell work. The class, engaged in the "What is the water like in our river?" unit, begins each day with a bell-work task that is written on the whiteboard at the side of the room, a small task that typically takes three to five minutes to complete. Mr. Knott does this to reduce the potential for distractions while he takes attendance and to focus students on their activities for class. This particular bell work asks students to "identify your team's water quality test, and state what potential problems the test might reveal about the river." The classroom is organized into six sets of tables, with chairs placed around each set of tables, accommodating up to six students in each group. At the center of each table is a baking pan containing a large plastic beaker, a small yellow booklet, a laminated card, test tubes, a test-tube holder, and a set of prepackaged foil capsules, each labeled with the name of a different water quality test. A few seconds after the bell rings, Mr. Knox pulls the door shut just as a student is coming in; he tells her she needs to make sure she isn't late again as he walks to the cart at the front of the room, which contains his computer, a projector, and some notes.

"All right, everyone. Two more minutes to answer the bell work in your notebooks," Mr. Knox says as he moves to his computer. He looks around the room to see which seats are empty today and notes attendance on his computer. After that, he pulls a folder from his desk and walks to three of the students in the room, giving them a copy of the packet of worksheets that other students are working from. For each, he quietly explains, "You'll use this with your group during the day today, and you can check with your group members if you have questions about the contents."

"All right, we need to talk about your bell work before we begin our investigations today. Do I have any volunteers?"

A student from the front table to his left is the first to raise her hand. As the teacher acknowledges her, she stands and reports to the class: "Our group is testing dissolved oxygen first. If there isn't enough dissolved oxygen in the water, the fish and other animals in the creek probably aren't getting enough oxygen there, and they might go to a different part of the creek where levels are higher."

"Is that true? Shawn?"

Another student from the same table, just across from the girl, answers, "Yes it is, Mr. Knott. If the dissolved oxygen level is too low, there might not be certain kinds of fish because they can't breathe."

"Right!" says Mr. Knott. "So, when the rest of you follow Group C, which is starting with the dissolved oxygen test, you might want to check with Shawn or the rest of the group to make sure you know what they found for their sample, in case your data is too high or low. Why don't we check with Group B now. Group B, what test are you starting with? Sophia, will you speak for your group?"

A girl from the middle front table stands with her notebook and reads, "Our group is testing for phosphates. Excess phosphorus in streams and surface waters can cause accelerated plant growth and algae blooms, which then cause rapid oxygen depletion or eutrophication in the water. The end product is water with low dissolved oxygen which cannot support aquatic life, including certain fish, invertebrates, and other aquatic animals."

"All right, everyone. Sophia just gave you all the information you need for phosphates. Remember, that information, along with the steps you will take, is all in the booklet on your equipment trays. Remember to read through both the steps of the test *and* the explanation of what your results might mean if they are higher or lower than the average. That needs to be in your explanation on your investigation sheet. Are you all with me?"

Mr. Knott proceeds through the rest of the tables, ensuring that each group has reviewed its testing booklet and at times picking up this booklet from the closest table's tray of equipment to hold up and make a point. Then he comes over to the cart, pulls down a screen to cover the boardwork question, and pushes a button on the projector, which brings up an image from a PowerPoint presentation. The screen shows bulleted steps that tell each group to make sure to read the test process in the booklet and to have the group timekeeper track how long the mixing of the tablets with the water samples takes, "to make sure you get the right results."

"Now, remember that each group should just have one person from the group come up with your large beaker and get the water sample from me. The water I collected from the creek this morning is in the bucket, so please give me your beaker and I will fill it, since I have sterile gloves on. Use this to pour into any of your tests so you don't contaminate the water. And when you are done with the test, have one person check the next group before you start the next test, so that we don't have some groups getting ahead of schedule compared to others. And, when you are done with all of your tests for the day, you should check your group's findings with mine to see how accurate you were. So, do you all have your recorder and your sampling collector? (looks around the room). Okay . . . ready, set, start your investigations!"

Mr. Knott circles the room, making sure student groups are on task and that each group is following the correct procedure as they engage in the investigation. As groups finish their original test, they begin the next, and so on, working their way through the set of six tests and writing down results individually for each. Only a few of the student groups check each other's results—instead, they just write down responses on a single worksheet until, as the class is nearing an end, Mr. Knott calls the class to attention and states, "We have three minutes until the bell. You should check your results with the group next to you and make sure everyone's name from your group is on the sheet. I will check these with mine and let you know if our tests agree, and tomorrow we will discuss what this might mean for the creek that our samples were taken from. When you are done, leave your samples on your trays and put the trays back on your class's shelf so I can review what you have, clean up the materials, and dispose of the solutions."

Class the next day starts in a similar manner, but without the equipment on the tables and with a new bell-work question: "Was the water in Flower Creek healthy, or not? Explain using the data from yesterday's investigation." Class discussion follows similar procedures as well, using a method of questioning that Mr. Knott calls "Stand and Deliver," which requests responses from a few volunteers (or selected students) as a representation of group response. Consensus generally agrees with Mr. Knott, though a few discussions arise around the dissolved oxygen reading and the times required to get the desired color change.

Ms. Amari's Classroom

Evelyn Amari is a former elementary school teacher with twenty-six years of experience teaching at three different schools in Detroit, Michigan. She was shifted to a middle school classroom two years ago based on layoffs in her district and a certification that allows her to teach any subject in grades K–8 (an endorsement that no longer exists). Her school sits adjacent to a large park along the Rouge River, which is one of three waterways that her students investigate to better understand issues of water and water quality at three points during the year. This description comes from the last set of investigations, which she runs in late April.

Ms. Amari's classroom seems a bit disorganized at first glance, but on closer examination, it is simply overflowing with information coming in from multiple students. On the wall nearest the entrance to the room is a large bulletin board space, separated into three separate boards. At the center of the middle board, in large cutout letters, is the question, "What is the water like in our river?" On this board are pinned three sets of colored paper, seemingly emanating from this question. The set on the left centers on a cutout circle, on which is written, "What do we know about our river?" and a lot of smaller rectangles with writing from different students stating either facts about both the Rouge and Detroit Rivers, as well as Connor Creek, or questions about each. Below is a similar cutout, with the main question of "How do our rivers compare with other rivers in the world?" and many sheets of information with details about the Nile, Mississippi, and Yangtze Rivers and the Grand and Tahquemenon Rivers in Michigan, and a third set, with far fewer pieces and details, but centered on the question, "How does a river change during the year?" To the left is a large map of the Rouge River watershed, showing several pinpoints marking the testing sites used by the Environmental Protection

Agency, Michigan Department of Natural Resources, University of Michigan–Dearborn, and Friends of the Rouge conservation organization. To the right is a large sheet drawn into a table with dozens of columns and about 100 rows. Each column is tracked by date.

Just after the bell rings, Ms. Amari closes the door and stops to address the class.

"Good morning, everyone. So, who is on data duty this week for second hour? We need updates from last week all posted before we head out." She pauses and looks at a name on the board. "Makeyla, the board says you are our data person this week, so please check with Justin, who had data duty last week, and let's get updates on the board."

"Actually, Ms. Amari, I have everything on the board. Friends of the Rouge did not post their update since they had some technical problems, and the email from Mrs. White at Dearborn Academy said that they had to delay their testing to this week because of lightning last Thursday when they were supposed to go out. So we have everything, and I checked with Shay, and she's updated the wiki data page as well."

"Ahhh, thank you, Makeyla! Did we hear that, everyone? We are up-to-date on data, so I want all teams to either look at the board or look at the data page on our wiki. So, take the next four minutes in small groups to review data, and I am going to come around and check on what each team is planning for our data collection today. I want to know what trends you have seen in last week's data and what you think you might see today, both in the chemical tests and in benthic collection. Also, think about the weather over the past week—I want to know what you think is going to happen to water levels, turbidity, and pollutant concentrations."

Ms. Amari walks over to the first table to hear what student groups are discussing in preparation for their data collection. She doesn't talk at first, not wanting to interrupt the discussion taking place. But she does gesture to the team record keeper to make sure that she has prepped the materials for her group to complete during the testing process. Alisha, the record keeper for the group this week, is putting the last name on the different categories of notes that three of the five members of her team will be using to record observations, weather conditions, data from the water quality testing, and numbers of different bugs collected during the sampling period. She checks through the notes quickly and gives Ms. Amari a quick thumbs-up, noting that all team members have what they need, while her teammate Darryl is using the team's laptop to pull up both the wiki and a weather website the team had bookmarked the previous week. As record keeper, Alisha is no mere secretary, but rather the leader in facilitating group conversation and coordinating data. In this way, multiple sets of eyes are engaged in observation, taking notes, and checking data for errors along the way. Each person enters his or her data in the spreadsheets that will be reviewed by other teams, as well as by teams at other schools and three field scientists from the local watershed council and a nearby university. Alisha is also in charge of noting the discussion questions colleagues bring up during the visit to their testing site, questions that will be shared during class discussion the next day.

"So I have the wiki up, and it looks like both water levels and phosphates are up as of this morning at the Nine Mile test station, but they are normal at the Dearborn center. I don't get that," says Darryl, as he looks at Ms. Amari for a response. She shrugs and points to Taylor, another girl in the group.

"I bet it was those storms last night," says Taylor. "I was with my mom shopping at Twelve Oaks [Mall], and it was pouring when we came out. We had to run to the car. But when we went home, it was dry from Seven Mile on, and I didn't see any water on the road this morning by our house when we came to school, so I don't think we even got rain here."

"So, Darryl, do me a favor," says Ms. Amari. "Go to the weather map and let's see if Taylor is right about the storms. There are a couple weather stations set up in Southfield, as well as in Franklin and Birmingham north of us, and in our usual stations in Detroit, Dearborn, and down by the airport. I am going to check with the other groups, but when I am done, we'll ask the whole class about that, and I want you to have the weather data to share to see if we can figure that out before we go out. In the meantime, get half of your group to think about the phosphate levels as well. If more water is coming into the river, it would probably be taking some of the surface-level phosphate sources with it, so you should brainstorm some ideas about what those sources might be so that we can include that in our conversation and data checking." With that, Ms. Amari moves on to the next table, checking for readiness of the record keepers and listening in on the other conversations to see if others noticed the difference in data between these sites. She is also noting questions and which groups were ready in a simple journal she uses to keep track of class progress.

There are subtle differences between Mr. Knott's and Ms. Amari's classrooms—differences in the language used by teacher and students, differences in the ways work is structured, and differences in the way the unit question is framed within a larger conception of knowledge in the discipline (see Figure 3.4). Both teachers are on a journey to improve their practice for the sakes of their students, but one teacher has moved down the path to a greater extent by positioning students as part of a diverse, scholarly disciplinary community.

Figure 3.4. Comparison of Mr. Knott's and Ms. Amari's science classrooms.

	Mr. Knott's Classroom	Ms. Amari's Classroom
Product or Performance	Students displayed school-congruent work habits to report on water testing, ensuring they arrived at correct results and followed procedures.	Students used disciplinary work habits to collaboratively construct a poster display, a detailed data table, and daily reports around an ongoing water-testing initiative.
Individual or Collaborative Performance	Students worked in table groups of six. Expectation was that students would check results, comparing with another table group and comparing with the teacher's correct answers.	Students worked in five-member teams with a team laptop. Data collection was first checked for errors, then shared and reviewed by multiple teams—in the classroom, at other schools, and by local scientists.
Knowledge Development	Students developed procedural fluency and accuracy running water quality tests. Students prepared information to be used in future analysis work.	Students developed ways of collecting, synthesizing, and making sense of data, viewing it from multiple perspectives. Students had the opportunity to compare results across multiple contexts and teams, including those outside of the school.
Expertise Development	Students enacted a role to complete a knowledge-creating task in science. Students learned a process for accurately testing water.	Students applied a process for gathering and confirming the accuracy of data over time. Students inhabited project-based roles that helped them create and transfer knowledge.
Role of Teacher	The teacher set up the experiments; he assigned them to perform bell work and group work. He reminded students to read the booklet; he reviewed the steps in a PowerPoint presentation. He served as coach, aiming to make it possible for students to understand what they should do, how, and why.	The teacher asked key questions and facilitated the students' abilities to perform their roles and engage in the work of water quality testing. She acted as an almost invisible thinking partner, aiming to develop student thinking.

What's the Big Deal about Disciplinarity?

Some have argued that disciplines are disappearing in a problem- and design-based world. We disagree; instead, we think that in this technologically networked age, it becomes even more important to understand the specific lenses and frames for knowledge making in some depth, both to operate effectively in one or several domains and to bridge domains in order to "make sense." Disciplines are being used, deeply, in combination with other skill sets to generate new products and ways of working. Actually, we're seeing indications that definitions of literacy are changing to include both qualitative and quantitative ways of seeing; the ante is being upped yet again.

Disciplines versus Applied Fields and Professions

People working in applied fields or professions draw on multiple disciplines on purpose, along with a host of practices and routines that their professional communities have evolved in response to particular issues or problems most often addressed in their line of work. For instance, nurses draw on mathematics, the sciences, communications, sociology, and psychology at various times to accomplish their work with their patients (see Figure 3.5). They might double check a dose calculation and then communicate with family members through a conference and written notes. To accomplish this important and complex work, they are drawing on many different experiences and kinds of knowledge. And skilled communication is important—perhaps just as important as knowledge of medicine—in a situation like a family conference about a patient's condition.

Traditionally, people being prepared as teachers have a much stronger bead on disciplines than they do on applied fields or professions, but it has become clear that young learners can benefit from understanding how what they are learning in social studies or mathematics addresses problems and issues in fields or professions. By arranging for an internship, a service learning project, or a collaboratively planned course of study with components on a job site, teachers give students opportunities to see where the disciplines and the knowledge generated within these frames fit into the world. Again, partnerships with professional practitioners seem imperative in generating the kinds of learning opportunities needed for students to make sense of the world they are stepping into.

The Importance of the Knowledge-Making Edge of a Discipline

If your aim is to move toward the establishment of authentic disciplinary communities in your classroom, another key factor is being able to locate and communicate about what we're referring to as "the knowledge-making edge" of a discipline

Figure 3.5. Disciplines and related fields and professions.

Disciplines	Applied Fields or Professions
Mathematics—algebra, geometry, trigonometry, calculus	Engineering, accounting, construction
Science—physics, chemistry, biology	Medicine, farming
English/Communications—text production and criticism	Journalism
Social Studies—history, economics, psychology, sociology, political science	Politics, counseling, social work

or field. Where is new thinking going on? What are the cutting-edge experiments being explored by disciplinary doers and makers? What are the debates playing out within key journals, conferences, and meetings? Where does all of the knowledge get applied in the "making" of something concrete and publicly seen? It is relatively easy to show students the knowledge-making edge of English language arts. Walk into any bookstore or open your Amazon app and you are confronted with thousands of voices sharing their stories through novels, poems, plays, and other textual forms. All are writers—and writers are busily inventing new stories and new ways of representing their worlds. Not all of these texts are immediately accessible to secondary students, but quite a few will be.

But it is significantly more difficult in mathematics, for example, for teachers to find and share the knowledge-making edge with their students. It's not that mathematics has a shortage of unsolved problems; just check Wolfram MathWorld under Unsolved Problems for a beginning list: http://mathworld.wolfram.com/UnsolvedProblems.html. Rather, because finding and sharing the knowledge-making edge in this discipline is a matter of depth in mathematical background knowledge and in the processes for tackling mathematical inquiries, such work is difficult for secondary students. Even college students majoring in mathematics may not know enough about the discipline, its problems, and its ways of working to handle even a taste of the knowledge-making edge of mathematics. And very little of the materials available for, and stated goals of, secondary mathematics address the processes of knowledge making in mathematics, let alone the knowledge-making edge. However, we would argue that if the goal of learning in the disciplines is authenticity and, ultimately, independence in learning, we need to try much harder than we have so far to show students how knowledge making works.

How and Why Do We Show Students in Mathematics the Knowledge-Making Edge?

James Tuttle, Bob Moses, and Greg Budzban

Partnerships:
Local: Ypsilanti Public Schools; National Network: Algebra Project; University Partners: University of Michigan Secondary Mathematics Lab and Southern Illinois University

As previously mentioned, there appear to be relatively few examples of mathematics curricula and activities that show young students the edge of knowledge making in that discipline. However, one example stands out in our minds: Algebra Project founder Bob Moses and mathematics professor Greg Budzban took a recently solved mathematical problem, referred to as "The Road Coloring Problem," and figured out how to turn it into a curricular unit accessible to struggling ninth graders. The problem centers on synchronized instructions; Bob and Greg use it as an opportunity for students to grasp multiple ways of representing a mathematical problem (arrow diagrams, ordered pairs, directed graphs, points on a Cartesian coordinate system, etc.) and to understand that mathematicians move back and forth between these representations as they do their work. It also is a chance to grasp the concept of functions and to deepen understanding of the process of mathematizing everyday situations. At the Algebra Project curriculum portal, students can submit solutions to facets of the problem and new ways of representing it through writing and photographs. In addition, students and teachers can examine newspaper articles about the man who solved the problem, Ari Trahtman, and his nine-page proof published in *Israel Journal of Mathematics*, which could give a glimpse of the expert discourse used in such an activity. (For one example, see http://usatoday30.usatoday.com/tech/science/mathscience/2008-03-20-road-coloring-problem-solved_N.htm.)

Bob Moses, Mary Maxwell West, and Frank Davis describe how they see the problem being used with students:

> Students experience the problem by laying out on the floor "cities" made of three or more "buildings," connected by "roads" that can be traveled in only one direction (indicated by color Blue or Red). One student stands in each "building." The task for other students is to figure out what series of instructions (walk Blue or Red roads) will produce the outcome where all students end up in the same building at the same time. (2009, p. 246)

Probably not every student engaging in the curricular unit grasps how *real* the problem is; literally hundreds of mathematicians worked on it over the course of about thirty years. So when Algebra Project students are building cities and representing them through directed graphs and arrow diagrams, they are making some of the same disciplinary moves as mathematicians. This kind of work is important in every discipline if we understand that learners need to see and believe that they *can* potentially be doers of a discipline.

How Do We Show Social Studies/History Students the Scope of History and the Knowledge-Making Edge?

Social studies/history and science also have knowledge-making edges that can be revealed to secondary learners if we are willing to work together to develop approaches that make sense. One of the most fascinating examples we've ever seen of disciplinary depth in history and science—and in interdisciplinarity—is a project that aims to contextualize human thought and history, beginning with the history of the universe. The Big History Project (BHP), developed by British historian David Christian and history education professor and outstanding classroom teacher Bob Bain, in partnership with schools and teachers in the United States and Australia and funded by Bill Gates, is a problem-based, inquiry-driven online curriculum for high schools (see www.bighistoryproject.com). In another sense, it is a collaboratively developed adaptation of a college-level course, sometimes referred to as ZOOM history. As the developers say, "Big history weaves evidence and insights from many scientific and historical disciplines across 13.7 billion years into a single, cohesive, science-based origin story. . . . Big history challenges students to think critically and broadly and tries to ignite a passion for inquiry" (Big History Project, n.d., p. 3). Interestingly, the partnerships that have been involved in the development of the course materials have led to a rich set of video and text resources, so there is a way to bring multiple disciplinary perspectives right into classrooms without necessarily having to organize lots of formal classroom visits.

Course goals include:

- Create, defend, and evaluate a narrative of change over time and space.
- Evaluate how historical and scientific discoveries have changed our understanding.
- Deepen understanding of key historical and scientific concepts.
- Locate our place in the big history (BH) narrative; use thresholds to frame past, present, and future.
- Compare interdisciplinary approach of big history to other approaches.
- Use various disciplines to analyze, discuss, and justify claims.
- Conduct investigations by framing the problem, researching, evaluating evidence, and constructing explanations and arguments.
- Critically read, synthesize, and analyze primary and secondary texts.

In some BH classrooms, students research, generate, and create "Little Big Histories": short video accounts that focus on a particular event or artifact and trace its history to the roots.

To pilot big history, a high school history department registers for an online interface and participates in foundational professional development so that students can access the rich available resources. The department then partners with local school colleagues and engages with other teachers and departments across the country and around the world, both through face-to-face and online means. They will also be partnering with historians and history educators.

Projects like Big History and the Algebra Project's rendition of "The Road Coloring Problem" bring our attention to authentic disciplinarity in an important way: introducing the real processes and actual uses of disciplinary knowledge making so that our students can understand why they would ever want to dig deeper into a discipline. That said, teachers must realize yet again that this kind of work is indeed a journey—one that ultimately can unfold over the course of multiple years for a teacher, in partnership with students and colleagues within and beyond a school or district.

Collegial Conversations: What are the real processes and actual uses of disciplinary knowledge making?

1. Identify a discipline, subject, or field you know and begin filling out the following template. What seems self-evident? What do you need to learn more about? What implications do you see for revising classroom practice?

Technical Language	
Big Questions	
Processes	
Knowledge-Making Edge	
Habits of Mind	

2. Return to the science vignettes of Mr. Knott's and Ms. Amari's classrooms. Reread them, looking for differences in stance and in classroom participation structures. What kind of learning experiences might help a teacher move from a more traditional teacher-directed science classroom to a disciplinary community structure?

3. Review the "edge of the discipline" examples, describing the "Road Coloring" mathematics problem and the Big History social studies course. What do you think is meant by "edge of the discipline"? What does this idea have to do with disciplinary learning communities?

Creating Opportunities for Disciplinary Talk

Specialist language varieties, whether the language of video gamers or of physicists, are technologies, just like computers, televisions, or phones. Technologies are tools that allow us to do certain things.

A variety of studies have shown that, in peer-peer discourse, children are less likely to defer to the authority of the other's viewpoint, more likely to seek some rational way to deal with differing viewpoints and perspectives, and more likely to actually change their own viewpoints for reasons they understand. . . .

—James Paul Gee, *Situated Language and Learning*

In the previous two chapters, we focused on the key teaching and learning practices of understanding expert performance and taking on disciplinary lenses. In this chapter, we examine ways in which teachers across the continuum of disciplinary literacy learning integrate opportunities for student talk. After years of teaching, observing, and collaborating in classrooms, we have come to the conclusion that students who have opportunities to engage in powerful talk as doers and makers in the disciplines begin to develop identities that lead them to act with agency. If, as Gee indicates, language is a technology and tool in disciplines and other specialized spaces, it is imperative that students have thoughtfully structured opportunities to acquire it. Learners grow as they engage in activities in which talking, reading, writing, and interacting lead them to value something—an idea, a cause, a topic—that makes who they are visible. Such language-in-use creates a discourse and space in which learning occurs, but this space also develops students' identities as doers of a way of thinking and/or being (Gee, 2004; Erickson, 2004).

For an illustration of what we mean, let's return to the Algebra Project for a moment. The practitioners and researchers involved with the Algebra Project recognize the importance of actually "talking math" in the context of classrooms, especially for students who are struggling. Algebra Project classrooms tend to be arranged so that students collaborate in small groups, talking about the problems they are working on. Groups eventually are called on to give informal presentations, laying out for their classmates problems and conjectures or conclusions on chart paper, as well as verbal explanations of the meaning and process. Algebra Project teachers also look for opportunities for their students to engage with outside audiences through more formal presentations, recognizing that these situations push students to polish their thinking and work and signal that math is important outside of the classroom, too. What's more, some of the Algebra Project curricular materials are designed so that students literally read "dialogues" between "mathematicians" and "students" out loud. In these dialogues, students are drawn out of everyday language by being given scripts for "speaking math." Here's an example of this kind of dialogue, taken from the Algebra Project's Trip Line materials (Dubinsky & Moses, 2010):

Student 1: What are we going to do with all our observation sentences about the Trip Line?

Mathematician: We are going to mathematize them.

Student 2: How do we do that? Is there a special way that we do that?

Mathematician: There are many ways to mathematize observation sentences. We are going to learn a way that uses the representations we have made. [Figure 4.1 represents the classroom chart that lists the types of features to be mathematized.]

Figure 4.1. Classroom chart of features.

Types of Features

- People and objects
- Actions
- Relationships

Student 3: I remember this.

Mathematician: Right! First we will just do observation sentences that show how two things are related. We will call these sentences Type A observation sentences.

Student 1: What kind of relations will we have?

Mathematician: For now, our relations will be that one landmark is to the left or to the right of another landmark. They are qualitative relations and don't involve any numbers.

Student 2: And they only involve the first and third features. What about actions?

Mathematician: Yes, that is so for Type A sentences. Type B sentences, which we will mathematize next, involve both actions and numbers, so they are quantitative relations.

Here, the curriculum materials put precise language in the mouths of young learners. In this way, students try on the language and, therefore, the mathematical thinking. This work is very different from giving students a list of math vocabulary words to memorize. As students talk and do the activity, they take up the language and use it to make sense and direct their work. As a result, students eventually connect language with the skills and habits of mathematicians and mathematics.

Situating Students to Develop Language in the Field

Dick Moscovic and Duane Olds, Construction Trades
Oakland Schools Technical Campus Northwest

Partnerships: Local Network: Oakland Schools Technical Campuses; State Network: Michigan Construction Trades Association (MCTA); Regional Network: Oakland Writing Project (OWP); Community Partnerships: City of Auburn Hills–Hawkwoods Nature Center, The Well, Grace Centers of Hope, etc.

Dick and Duane, whose work was introduced in Chapter 2, both own construction companies and use the language of construction trades in their day-to-day lives with multiple audiences: a range of tradespeople who work for them, clients, and salespeople. When they step into the classroom, they use the same language with their students. When we asked them about classroom talk, they suggested that onsite learning is essential and precise language is important when teaching, because when many of the students leave the classroom they move directly to jobs in construction trades. The language used onsite is the language they will use to talk to their future boss, explain the work to clients, or order supplies for a job. Dick explains:

> Visualization is essential to understand what is being built and how to build it. The language Duane and I use with students has to create a verbal portrait in the students' minds. When we talk to students, we are thinking about the image the words create. We try to make an analogy and connect the current work to previous experiences. We describe explicit actions and name specific tools and materials. Then the words we share in conversations become the way students visualize the task and think about the work while doing it. If we put a saw in a student's hand and he cuts the material short, it is not the student's fault. We anticipate errors. Errors are part of the educational journey. Until a student sees the finished product or makes mistakes and sees the error, the language doesn't mean much. Ripping out a mistake is a valuable learning experience. Whether our coaching translates to quality work or repair of an error, students are learning to build to an industry standard. Sometimes mistakes create more permanent lessons when students talk about what went wrong and plan how to repair the problem. Students' identities as tradespeople and the quality of the work increase as students increase their ability to talk about the work and problem-solve in conversations with each other.

To observe and understand the position Dick takes when he talks with his students, we stopped at Dick's onsite classroom one sunny afternoon in May. His

students were immersed in the rehabilitation of a house in downtown Pontiac, Michigan, that would become an after-care residence for clients of Grace Centers of Hope drug abuse and addiction facility. This onsite classroom situates the students as tradespeople with a client and a city assessor who evaluates their work against city, county, and state codes. The job presented a significant challenge since the house was built in the 1920s and had fallen into disrepair over the last ninety years. As a result, many areas of the house were not square, level, or plumb. Although the house passed inspection for habitation, the renovations would make the house livable by current standards.

Dick and Duane were extremely aware of the accurate use of foundational language and the importance of talk to think through and solve the complex problems presented by this renovation project. For example, the foundational language of *plumb*, *level*, and *square* served as a guide for planning and self-assessment for everything built in the shop or on a new construction site. However, on this rehab site, students used the foundational language to assess the site before they problematized the situation and planned a solution. This required them to develop a sophisticated working vocabulary and an ability to visualize the process first in words. In this situation, students reached the limits of foundational language of one field in construction trades and pushed beyond terms used in rough carpentry, such as *header*, *trimmer*, or *crippler stud*, into vocabulary used in the specific field of trim carpentry, with terms such as *miter*, *cope*, *bevel*, and *crown mold*, and the field of aluminum trim construction, with terms such as *coil*, *fascia*, *frieze*, and *soffit*. These shifts also required students to use knowledge and vocabulary of applied geometry, such as *Pythagorean theorem*, *hypotenuse*, *angle*, *degree*, *circumference*, *parallel*, and *perpendicular*. For example, students had to find the hypotenuse of the corners of the footings for the home in order to square the foundation. If a carpenter's square, tape measure, and construction calculator are not handy, they might use the Pythagorean theorem. The same mathematical principle

would be used to square a wall before applying the required covering to it. In this renovation, students were determining the degree of the internal angle to cut and fit siding on the gable end of the house.

As students ripped away walls to uncover the construction standards of 1920, they needed a working language for today's standards to talk about the differences in construction and the multiple processes they would use to make decisions on next steps as they devised a plan of action for the renovation. The language-in-use increased the knowledge students gained about construction standards and the hands-on skills they gained identifying multiple solutions for the problems the house presented.

When we arrived, teams at all levels of expertise were working on various tasks: one team mudded drywall, a second team installed and trimmed interior doors, and a third installed vinyl soffits and fascia. As usual, Dick assigned the work teams and met with each team to review the work and coach students. Immediately we noticed he talked to the teams in different ways. For example, he coached the drywall repair team by working side by side in a step-by-step instructional voice. Then he left so that students could independently apply the techniques he had just modeled and guided them through. Later, he checked back to facilitate self-assessment, or in some cases to describe why the work did not meet industry standard and how to repair or redo it. In contrast, he took the position of boss as he

talked to the door installers, who were into their third day of installing and preparing to trim the interior doors. He asked them to estimate the wood they needed to complete the trim job so that he could order materials for the morning crew. Then he moved on to Eric, who was installing aluminum trim on the porch. With Eric, Dick chose to take the position of thinking partner. Figure 4.2 captures a brief conversation between Dick and Eric that allows them to think out loud together.

Figure 4.2. A thinking partner conversation.

Dick's Thinking Partner Conversation with Eric

Dick: How are you going to address the situation to wrap this beam?

Eric: I want to do it in two pieces. Not one. [*Pauses and looks at another beam already wrapped in aluminum.*] That last one was difficult. I had to cut a lot off the other piece. It took too long. Wasted a lot of stock figuring it out.

Dick: [*Pauses and looks at the beam to be wrapped.*] Well, you could create a template for each end of the beam since they are different dimensions. Then create an overall measurement so you combine the templates to fit the entire beam.

Eric: I don't know. I understand my way. [*Pauses and looks at the beam to be wrapped.*] I know I can bend the stock to fit with very few cuts if I use two pieces of stock.

Dick: [*Pauses.*] Go ahead. It has to be acceptable to the eye when you finish capping the other side.

Eric: Sure.

Dick: You'll need to create a smash trim to cover the raw edge so it appears finished.

Eric: Not sure about the smash. That is for later.

Dick: Okay. Try it your way, and shout when in doubt. Advice is free.

From the position of thinking partner, Dick used his knowledge of the situation: Last week a team of students had dismantled the previous porch, which

hung at a 60° angle from the front door, and replaced it with a porch that was square, level, and plumb; however, the roof over the porch was not square or level to the new porch. The client did not plan on ripping off and replacing the roof over the porch. Eric faced significant problems in making and installing aluminum trim out of coil stock. For the trim to look acceptable, Eric needed to use his knowledge of conventional trimming on new construction to solve the problems of this situation. Dick anticipated errors, but he also knew that Eric could think his way through the complex installation and develop new thinking and vocabulary in making the trim.

Instead of modeling or coaching as he did with the drywall team, Dick engaged Eric as an equal and allowed Eric to explore an alternate plan and make the final decision. He also offered a standard that was achievable, "acceptable to the eye" and "appears finished." Trim would not repair the out-of-square roof beam; however, carefully applied, it would visually hide the problems and be acceptable for this renovation. As a thinking partner, Dick became an activator of Eric's thinking and allowed Eric, who tends to be quiet, to think through the task out loud but also think through his own limitations to accomplish it. With this awareness, Dick left Eric with several suggestions that Eric at first seemed to be rejecting.

As Eric worked, he thought aloud and reflected on the difficulty of the approach to the task he had planned even though he thought creating two pieces would be easier. He stated that he enjoyed having the choice and the opportunity to try it his way. He incorporated some of the shared thinking as he created a piece of trim appropriate for an in-square beam, and then he fitted, measured, cut, and fitted the trim again before installing it. After the first half was installed, he said, "I love that my way works." In the end, he revised his thinking and planned how to attach the trim to the soffit. He explained, "That took a lot longer than I thought. This work is slow with all the measuring and remeasuring to adjust for the problem."

After he trimmed one side of the beam, Eric noticed that the trim on the beam he had finished yesterday was bowing out; it would have to be repaired. He said, "If it was me, and I was doing this for someone's house, I'd have to fix this with my own money." His comment suggests he understood that time and errors cost money, and he needed to learn how to do things quickly and accurately in any situation.

Later, when Dick returned, Eric explained how he was going to install the trim on the outer side of the beam. He would stick the bend into the J-channel on the overhang trim and caulk the flat side. But he was not sure about the smash. As before, Dick and Eric thought through the installation options and planned the task together.

Let's pause to return to the continuum of disciplinary literacy learning. Figure 4.3 summarizes the roles, actions, and disciplinary talk that illustrates learning that occurs in the Authentic section of the continuum.

At the end of the semester, Eric and Craig, the young man who mudded the ceiling, wrote reflective essays about the impact of learning "from the fingertips back." Each pointed out how authentic work and an environment that values learning through conversations impacted their expertise and their identity as competent individuals. Eric, who now works on the maintenance crew of a local municipality, wrote:

Figure 4.3. Developing language in the field.

	Situating Students to Develop Language in the Field
Product or Performance	Eric learned how to wrap the porch in aluminum trim. The porch was out of square and presented problems that required Eric to adjust his knowledge of trimming learned in new construction.
Individual or Collaborative Performance	Although Eric worked alone, Dick opened the conversation with an open-ended question (*How are you going to address the situation to wrap this beam?*) that allowed Eric to function as an equal in a collaborative conversation. Eric reflected on this conversation as he worked, and he referenced it when Dick returned to check in on Eric's progress.
Knowledge Development	The conversation provided Eric with an opportunity to retrieve and apply knowledge from recent work to a similar but slightly more complex task. In the conversation, Dick listened and assessed Eric's knowledge and misconceptions so that he could provide feedback. Eric needed to think several steps beyond his knowledge and experience. The talk left Eric with clarity about what he knew and what he would learn.
Expertise Development	Eric set into action his alternate plan. As we watched him, he paused to think to himself. This self-talk slowed him down but also helped him test his approach before he made the next measurement or cut. He understood this work would devise a system to apply to the next two beams. He also found himself evaluating the first beam to anticipate steps to increase the quality of his work, which eventually led him to decide to redo the first beam.
Role of Teacher	Dick took the role of thinking partner that positioned Eric as an expert and equal in their conversation. It also activated Eric's thinking and empowered Eric to "do it his way." Dick closed the conversation with a choice to ask for clarification within a system that accepted confusion.

Working as a tradesman allowed me to improve my communications skills by constantly talking with Coach. Our talks helped me get my thoughts out of my head and work through problems, slow down, and advance my skills. He gave me advice, but he also gave me the green light to make my own decisions. After the talks to plan together, I did the work with Coach's thinking and words in the back of my head. Working hands-on also boosted my confidence. In a regular classroom, I took a test, got a lot of answers wrong, and got a bad grade. Onsite I learned from my mistakes. Coach always said, "First time is for practice" and in some cases it was 1, 2, 3 times for practice. Talking with Coach when I planned or when I screwed up was one of the best ways to learn because it allowed me to make adjustments and improvements to my approach.

Craig, who now attends college in the Construction Management Program, wrote:

Coach Moscovic talked to me with respect and the same way I would eventually talk on a job site. He corrected me so I sounded professional, but he also made it easy to ask questions when I didn't know what to do. Over time everyone onsite picked up on a way of talking to each other. We spoke with more detail so we could better understand what we wanted or what needed to be done effectively. I learned specific talk makes work more efficient. Now, I talk with the clear detail I learned to use onsite when I am communicating with a range of people in lots of different settings.

The visit to Dick's site raised questions for us about the shifts teachers in traditional classroom settings will face as they design disciplinary learning experiences. As we watched Dick move quickly from room to room engaging students in a variety of instructional conversations, a question emerged: How does a teacher create spaces for substantial conversations with students and between students in a traditional classroom? We asked Dick to explain his system for teaching in an environment that requires students to work both in teams and independently while they self-monitor their work. Dick explains:

> I like to start and end each day one to one with my students. So they know they shake hands with me and have a private conversation when they arrive and before they leave. The rest of the half-day session is focused conversations. Occasionally, the whole class is engaged in one activity such as pouring foundations, but typically students work in teams in different areas of the house. This reduces traffic, provides a more authentic work space, and enables focused task completion. A typical half-day session is broken into four overlapping parts: (1) huddle up and focus; (2) team and/or individual work with coaching; (3) pause for problem solving; and (4) check in and assess. I move from team to team, coaching students to explain their work or imagine solutions for problems that occur or are created in the learning process.

On the afternoon we watched Dick, his instruction followed the routine he describes, which is illustrated in more detail in Figure 4.4. Later we talked with Duane, who explained that he uses similar routines because his construction shop has five rooms, and his students also work in teams in various areas of the shop. He explained that he moves from group to group, always assessing ways to support students so they can accomplish the work independently. He often works side by side with students for brief periods to serve as a model or to demonstrate a way to use a tool. Figure 4.4 describes the focus for talk during typical lesson architecture for onsite construction trades.

Watching and learning from these construction trades students and instructors have led us to wonder how their approaches to talk might transfer to other subject area classrooms. Let's immerse ourselves next in the classrooms of a team of English teachers whose focus on increasing student talk in develop disciplinary learning led to a significant shift in practice.

Figure 4.4. Disciplinary talk in a construction class session.

Focus of Disciplinary Talk in a Typical Construction Class Session		
Part of Session	**Summary of Teacher and Student Actions**	**Focus of Talk**
Huddle Up and Focus	Students greeted and shook hands with Dick upon arriving onsite. They engaged in a one-to-one discussion of the work accomplished by the a.m. crew and the focus and scope of the work assignment for the day.	• Shifted students to role of tradespeople, assigning job or team. • Discussed the focus, problem, or goal for learning. • Asked questions to assess level of independence.
Team and Individual Work with Coaching	Students collected tools, set up their work space, and began work. During this setup time, Dick pulled individuals or full teams together to talk through the work plan (door installation) or guide students in an essential habit and process (measuring and cutting in fascia installation). He also met one-to-one with individuals starting a new process (drywall repair). As students worked, Dick moved from team to team throughout the session, coaching in a variety of ways based on student need (siding installation). He returned multiple times to each team.	• Coached step-by-step directions as student tried new task. • Served as thinking partner to activate problem solving for multiple solutions to develop self-efficacy. • Played role of crew chief as students played role of tradespeople. • Observed and listened as students self-assessed and provided feedback on their work.
Pause for Problem Solving	Dick anticipated errors and planned time to return for reflection and refocusing. Based on feedback gained through student conversations, he identified groups for more frequent drop-in support. Novice learners needed support in the use of tools, step-by-step processes for routine tasks, development of assessment skills, and application of industry standards. Experienced learners faced challenges that required problematizing the task and systematizing the process.	• Modeled tool usage to increase accuracy and adjust ineffective work habit. • Served as a thinking partner to assess and systematize learning gained from current methods for future work.
Check in and Assess	Students cleaned their work area and put the tools into the school van or trailer. They shook hands with Dick and discussed the work accomplished that day. In this brief self-assessment moment, students recalled strengths or problems they resolved. Some students asked questions about at-home construction projects. The check-in ended with collaborative identification of a goal for tomorrow's work.	• Engaged in personal conversation with each student. • Listened as students self-assessed the work they accomplished. • Coached application of onsite learning to at-home construction projects. • Collaboratively set a goal for tomorrow's work for some students.

Developing Roles and Spaces for Disciplinary Talk and Language Use

Peter Haun, Carissa Peterson, Katie Locano, and Steven Snead
English Department, Oak Park High School

Partnerships: Department: Study Team; State Network: School Improvement Grant (SIG); Regional Network: Oakland Writing Project (OWP); National Network: National Writing Project (NWP) and Learning Design Collaborative (LDC)

After receiving a School Improvement Grant (SIG) and undergoing major school restructuring, Oak Park High School (OPHS) faced the challenge of accelerating the learning and achievement of students with significant struggles in reading and writing. If students did not make significant growth, the school faced closure. Five English language arts teachers—Peter Haun, Katie Locano, Carissa Peterson, Ann Rzepka, and Steven Snead—took the lead in shifting their instructional practices from *doing school* to *doing the discipline*. They partnered with Linda, who facilitated the change process and served as a classroom coach.

If you had stepped into any of their classrooms in 2010, most would have been similar to Steven's senior-level ELA class. He loves literature, especially Shakespeare. He wants his students to love it as much as he does. When Linda observed him teaching *Othello* in May of 2010, Steven supported his students by preparing engaging and entertaining lectures with carefully paired clips from the play, as well as brief readings from the text. Occasionally he asked a question and then talked through the confusions that emerged in student answers in one-to-one conversations with a single student while other students listened. His students loved his class, and they gained an appreciation for Shakespeare and other canonical texts that they would not be able to read independently. But when the team began observing one another in the fall of 2010, Steven's statement echoed those of his colleagues: "I didn't realize how much I talked."

Realizations like this fueled three important shifts that occurred early in the school year and developed spaces for students to engage in disciplinary talk: (1) teachers positioned students in the *role of writer* and adopted the *role of fellow writer* and coach in a community of writers; (2) teachers designed daily tasks to increase rigorous *turn and talk conversations* in which students learned and applied disciplinary language; and (3) teachers revised their *lesson architecture* to create opportunities for students to talk every day.

Role of Writer

From the beginning, OPHS teachers stepped into the role of writer and embraced the value of creating writing communities. In September they launched their writing communities with authentic doing and making of personal narratives. As the teachers created classroom communities, students engaged in the habits of writers and focused on writing for publication; they shifted from being doers of writing assignments and began to see themselves as writers and creators of texts. As fellow writers, teachers focused on modeling the explicit writerly language that became the tool of thinking and sharing.

However, teachers faced two challenges as they shifted into their role as fellow writer and increased writerly conversations in classrooms. First, they felt uncomfortable talking about their writing with students. It seemed easier (and safer) to examine and discuss student writing. Second, they needed to learn more about the habits, strategies, and processes of writing genres they had never written before. To respond to these challenges, teachers met monthly to write together. They engaged in writer response groups, which helped them to develop explicit language to explain their thinking and decision making and to identify the decisions of fellow teacher-writers in the group. By talking as writers, they immersed themselves in the explicit disciplinary language that they wanted their students to learn. Maintaining the role of writer when they stepped into classrooms, they conveyed to their students that writing is not about luck or following a recipe. Rather, it is about focused, experimental, recursive work and decisions in a discursive community of writers.

After teaching their first authentic writing unit, Peter noted, "I have come to value a classroom community because it makes a huge difference. It encourages students to talk more and take risks in those conversations." Ann added, "Students enjoy sharing their writing. They are learning more about each other as they read aloud personal stories to each other." Carissa said, "Students enjoy making decisions and talking about the choices they make to plan and craft their writing." Katie concluded, "When I share my writing and talk about my decisions as a writer, my students see me as a partner in the work. We are all writers in a community of writers."

In this new role of writer, teachers and students shifted from knowers of content to students of the habits, strategies, processes, and thinking that writers who publish personal narratives use. Today, every OPHS English teacher starts the year with a unit that establishes a community of writers and develops a common language, student identities as writers, and student agency.

Turn and Talk Conversations

As Linda coached their work with student writers, the teachers realized that dialogue is essential in a writing community. Language on the page or in the air drives the work of individual writers and builds their identities as well as the aesthetic of the community. Writers need an explicit common language, opportunities to talk, and literacy practices that increase uses for talk and that shift tasks so that they encourage critical thinking, elicit multiple views, and engage students in problem solving.

The term *turn and talk* clearly names the action—turn and face a partner—and the task—talk in a specific way. Often OPHS teachers assigned turn and talk partners, and students stayed with that partner for an entire unit or a designated period of time. Student partners may talk to make sense of a task, to try a strategy, to reflect on their work, to share and compare points of view on a topic or reading, or to solve a problem. Routine turn and talk conversations center on students using three basic disciplinary literacies in reading and writing literature:

- **Reading like writers**—reading to notice, name, and create theories about texts; reading to research and study the craft and structural decisions that are universal across genres and unique to a specific genre; reading to understand the constraints and opportunities in a genre

- **Writing as decision makers**—writing with persistence and stamina to grow knowledge of the craft and structure of a genre; writing to mentor and experiment with craft and structural decisions and independently apply them to their writing throughout the writing process

- **Talking to share, reflect, and explain**—engaging in conversations to read aloud and share their writing, to reflect on or explain their processes and choices, or to listen and respond to other writers using writerly language

As a community of practice emerged, so did students' abilities to communicate alternative perspectives and alternate ways of seeing and understanding (Gee, 2004; Tomasello, 1999) the texts of published authors, the texts of peers and the teacher, and the texts they were writing and revising. Steven Snead noticed that giving students strategies and time to talk and make sense of these strategies increased their independence, engagement, and ownership of the writing.

Framing conversations around use of disciplinary habits and language changed the interactions in the room. Students acted, talked, and used language to drive their doing and making of texts. Ultimately, this also changed the design of the teachers' daily lessons.

Lesson Architecture

Increasing opportunities for substantive conversations was at the heart of shifting to workshop lesson architecture. It provided more time for students to talk using disciplinary language and processes. It also required teachers to design authentic independent tasks that positioned students as doers of the discipline for most of the class period.

Although OPHS teachers struggled to let go of control, they continued to expand their instructional repertoire as they became more committed to opening spaces for students to talk as writers making decisions with a reader in mind. They agreed to shorten their lessons and to model and think aloud for students using explicit language. In this way, students had time to talk to one another in focused conversations multiple times during the class period. Teachers used these student conversations to listen in on student thinking both as they talked and on the page, providing an opportunity to assess student uptake of the lesson and use of disciplinary knowledge. The lesson architecture also gave teachers regular spaces in each hour to talk with students and assess and support day-to-day changes and watch growth over time (Calkins, 1994; Zemelman, Daniels, & Hyde, 2012). As a daily approach to learning, it also functioned as a gradual release of responsibility toward independent performance in each daily lesson and in a series of lessons within a unit of study (Wilhelm, Baker, & Dube, 2001; Calkins, 1994, 2010; Zemelman, Daniels, & Hyde, 2012).

OPHS teachers used two routine architectures for lessons that increased use of disciplinary language in teacher talk and opened spaces for students to talk and use the language that teachers modeled. Both routines included the following parts:

Mini-Lesson

- Teacher models and thinks aloud explicit habit, process, or strategy with explicit disciplinary language to develop a repertoire of ways of thinking, reading, writing, and talking.
- Students turn and talk to rehearse and think aloud the habit, strategy, or process.
- Teacher clarifies application of habit, process, or strategy prior to independent work based on listening to student turn and talk conversations.

Independent Work

- Students enact the habit, process, or strategy as they continue with their independent work.
- Teacher confers briefly with students, moving around the room to serve as a coach, fellow writer, and/or thinking partner.

- Peers may talk briefly, serving as a coach or fellow writer to discuss use and impact of decisions they are making.

Sharing/Reflecting

Sample of options:

- Read aloud parts of a working draft in trios so partners can serve as critical friends to notice an important decision point in the writing that was a strength, to recall or point to the exact words on the page, to name the craft or structure, and to explain the impact of the decision on the reader.
- Turn and talk to respond to a reflective prompt. Gather and use evidence from current work in the responses.
- Turn and talk to examine and respond to a student sample that serves as a model. Discuss the evidence in the sample to support conclusions about the text.

Adopting these elements for their lesson architecture, the OPHS team decreased and focused teacher talk and found spaces for substantive student conversations.

In May of this first year of change, the teachers reflected on their shifts in teaching and learning. Peter noted:

> Now, we try to instruct in manageable chunks and adjust that instruction in "real time." This type of modeling positions the teacher as a fellow community member. Not the perfect keeper of knowledge. I've found students tend to trust you more when you put yourself in front of the class as a vulnerable writer, someone who is willing to make mistakes. And because students use and talk about these manageable chunks, we begin to share a common way of talking about our work, and they internalize smaller concepts before we move on to the bigger ideas. Many of the students don't have an academic identity or language. So acquiring the language around small concepts quickly accelerates the learning, diminishes the struggles and confusion, and gradually builds an identity as a competent reader or writer.

Katie noted:

> Some of the students who I might have thought "don't get it" made some really bright suggestions to others when we did response groups and peer conversations. This also makes me think that I've been doing too much explaining because I expect kids won't get it. What I need to do is break things down along the way because they can understand and use the specific strategies and habits of published writers. Maybe I need to explain less and model those strategies and habits more.

Let's pause to return to the continuum of disciplinary literacy learning. Figure 4.5 summarizes the roles, actions, and disciplinary talk that illustrate learning that occurs in the Foundational and Project-Based sections of the continuum.

Figure 4.5. Disciplinary talk and language use.

	Developing Roles and Spaces for Disciplinary Talk and Language Use
Product or Performance	Study and adopt the habits, strategies, and processes of published writers to generate, experiment, draft, revise, and edit a narrative, memoir, or poem for publication beyond school.
Individual or Collaborative Performance	Develop routine ways of talking and using language to engage in turn and talk conversations. This talk provides alternate views on a text, positioning students as fellow writers, critical friends, and problem solvers. Engaging in conferences with teacher and peers instigates critical thinking and reflection.
Knowledge Development	Develop basic disciplinary literacy practices: reading like a writer, writing as a decision maker, and talking to share, reflect, or explain. Develop a common language for decisions writers make in a narrative genre and the process of writing across time.
Expertise Development	Adopt the role of writer and critical friend in a writing community. Develop, retrieve, and apply a repertoire of habits, strategies, and processes to write and read that can be transferred to another text and/or genre.
Role of Teacher	Design and initiate explicit dialogues that provide an opportunity for students to use disciplinary language, habits, and processes. Serve as a fellow writer, model, and coach in a community of writers.

Developing Disciplinary Social Practices

Laura Mahler
English Department, Clarkston High School

Partnerships: Clarkson High School English Department; Regional Network: Oakland Writing Project (OWP); National Network: National Writing Project (NWP) and Literacy Design Collaborative (LDC).

Laura Mahler, whose classroom work was introduced in Chapter 2, situates her students as writers through a social practice used by published writers—writer response groups. Her students engage in writer response groups frequently throughout the year and across the generating, experimenting, drafting, revising, and editing process. Here are some of Laura's recommendations:

> Get students into response groups early and often. Early response can provide new thinking and open avenues in the text that the writer had not considered. Also, when students are writing longer texts, it is beneficial for them to bring a chunk of the text [to the group]. Some reasons students select a chunk might be (1) the writer has carefully structured a passage and wants confirmation on the effectiveness of the reasoning or sequence of passage; (2) a writer finds a passage troublesome and wants alternate ways to solve a problem; or (3) a writer may be too close to a story and needs an outside reader to identify what is clearly on the page and what is still in the writer's head.

Laura's students use several slightly different response group protocols as students gain skill across the year or as they shift back and forth from authentic genres, when they write poetry, short fiction, memoir, or screenplays, to academic genres, when they write literary explication essays and practice prompt writing required on the Advanced Placement Literature exam.

Writer response groups pass the authenticity test. A common practice of published writers from a wide range of disciplines and genres is to read their work and listen to their group members serving as early readers as they make sense of and analyze the craft and structure of a text. Note that these response group members do not serve as editors fixing the text or recommending changes.

For students, response groups serve the same purpose, and in doing so, the groups become a vehicle for understanding the discipline of writing and taking up disciplinary language. Like expert writers, student group members agree on a protocol for polite but critical response. Several classroom protocols are identical or similar to response protocols used by published authors. They range from simple to more complex and include Richard Koch's "Praise, Question, Suggest (PQS)" (1982); the National Writing Project's "Bless, Address, or Press" (n.d.); Stephen Dunning's "Writer Response Group Protocol" (Bencich, 1997, Appendix B); and National School Reform Faculty's "Critical Response Process Protocol" (McKean, 2013).

Writer response group conversations achieve more than feedback for a writer. They go beyond peer review, which might focus too heavily on error and not enough on strength and on noticing the craft and structure that invents and supports the meaning(s) in a text. Focused in this way, the conversation stays in the realm of sense making and analysis by readers who are knowledgeable writers. The readers (who are also writers) in a group talk to one another. The writer becomes an eavesdropper, and the overheard conversation gives the writer (who stays silent and outside of the conversation) the gift of listening in on several readers as they notice, name, and explain what stands out; how the writing is created; what it means or might mean or could mean with changes. Although these readers may at some point make suggestions for change or clarity, the major part of the group conversation provides the writer with an inside view of a reader's head.

Key to this approach is the belief that the writing belongs to the writer who has crafted it. The group might provide confirmation that the writer communicates clearly; the group might see the characters or story line in an unexpected way; and as readers point out the details they connected, the writer has the opportunity to hear this new way of reading the text. If the group makes suggestions, they are spoken *as* suggestions. Thus, the writer does not leave the group with a list of things to fix, such as "add details here" or "take this part out because it is confusing." Instead, the writer has information that she or he can use to shape future writing and possible revisions. The focus is on the writer and the decisions visible in the text. It is not on "correctness" of the writing.

It takes time for students to develop the reading and conversational language for highly effective response groups. Readers develop the skills to be thoughtful noticers, connecters, and explainers of details, craft, and structural decisions in a text. They also develop as critical listeners to the other readers with whom they may agree or disagree as the conversation around a text progresses. Writers also need to be critical listeners and note takers so that when they leave the group they can use the rich information they heard to consider their text with new eyes. Response groups focused in this way become a place where identity and agency can be developed through social practices—the ways writers talk and listen to one another.

On a cold, snowy day in January, we visited Laura's classroom to observe several writer response groups. At this point in the year, Laura's students were in Cycle II of their writing for publication unit, and they were at various stages of drafting and revising texts that would be submitted for publication beyond school. (See Chapter 2 for more details about the cycles of this class.) If you glanced around the room, you would see poets, memoirists, fiction writers, and screenplay writers.

One group, comprising three young women who wrote short fiction and a young man who wrote a screenplay, invited us to eavesdrop on their conversations. The group formed by pulling four desks together; passing copies of their writing clockwise around the group; and selecting a timer, a first reader, and an order for future readers. We stayed and listened to the group, making plans to return in a week when a second response group was scheduled. In this first group, students consciously worked to reduce their natural tendency to notice errors and make suggestions for change. Figure 4.6 is a transcript from the second response group. It captures the group's response to Jillian's short fiction piece written in the form of a diary. (See the appendix for drafts of Jillian's work, her response group reflection, and drafts from her response group partners, Amanda, Dylan, and Kristen, as well as their reflections.) Jillian came to the second group meeting with an almost complete draft. She selected part of the new writing to gather response from the group. Figure 4.6 is a conflated transcript of the group conversation that lasted eight minutes and fifty-two seconds. Writerly language has been boldfaced in the transcript.

Figure 4.6. Jillian's writing draft and writer response group reflections.

Jillian's Writer Response Group Conversation

Jillian: [*Before reading her piece aloud, she links today's work to last week's response group.*] I read the first two entries last time. I've added several. [*Flips through pages, then looks at Laura standing next to the group.*]

Laura: Which section of your draft do you want response on? What will be most helpful for you?

Jillian: The part that I added is September 3rd to September 9th. [*Reads several entries from a fictional diary about an international model who eats ice for days and engages in extreme exercise in order to fit into designer dresses for a fashion show. The final entries describe her observations after she wakes up in a hospital.*]

Amanda: [*Silence as all group members reread their notes. To Jillian,*] I like your use of **diction.** You use . . . [*Jillian stops her and points to the others to indicate that she is not in the conversation. Amanda pauses, then starts again, shifting her language to exclude Jillian.*] The author uses a lot of words like *empty* and *it's all their fault* and *they made it this way.* The **diction** made it seem that she was alone, and she was blaming others for her issues. And I think it helps contribute to the overall **theme** she is going for.

Kristen: Yeah, I noticed that in the different diary entries, she seems okay and knows what is wrong, and other times it seems like she blames them all for her starving herself. So I think it is like an **internal conflict** we are seeing in the character that we are seeing in her **diction** and how she says certain things.

Dylan: Yeah, I noticed, right here [*Pauses and points to a specific diary entry.*], the very first entry that she read . . . [*Kristen and Amanda flip to the entry.*], she makes **reference** to eating French food and thunder thighs. That is not what you usually think about when eating French food. It is usually small portions. So one doesn't usually think that way. And thunder thighs, you don't really think about that when you think about models. It gives you a different **point of view** on it—from a model's **point of view.**

Kristen: Yeah, it shows how upset she is about being fat and that she goes to extremes. It's an extreme thing, thunder thighs, and you know it isn't accurate. Thunder thighs.

Amanda: And to go along with that, almost every **entry ends** with *let's keep this between us* . . . or *whatever that means.* . . . It kind of leads you on to the **next entry** and I wonder . . . It makes me wonder what will happen to her because she is malnourished.

Kristen: Yeah, so, I think the author is trying to put it as if the diary is . . . **like the diary is a friend** to this girl because it isn't like she is talking to herself; it is almost like she is talking to a friend. [*Pauses.*] So the way she says, *let's keep it to between us* . . . it is like you were saying. . . .

Amanda: [*Extends Kristen's comment and adds details from the earlier entries read in last week's response group.*] Yeah. Even though she does say she has a friend that is on the cover of *Vogue*, it almost seems like she has no friends. All she worries about is her job and not eating. [*Long pause as all the group members reread notes.*] And she has good **parallel structure** with *to be strong* and *to be good.* [*Long pause as all the readers are flipping pages and rereading the diary.*] I think it is really interesting how she **separates each entry** with a date. And how many days she lets pass between each one. Like before she is in the hospital to the day she is in the hospital, two days pass. And it shows eleven days between the first entry of September 3 and the entries before that. So it's interesting how she separates each entry instead of having them day after day after day.

Kristen: Yeah. It makes it more realistic.

Jillian: [*Almost inaudibly thanks the group members.*] That idea came from a book I read as a sophomore that had a **line about the novel being** a story line of denial. So that **line really impacted me,** and I thought about that when I was writing.

Dylan: That's good. That's perfect.

Continued on next page

Figure 4.6. Continued.

Kristen:	[*Turns to Jillian and addresses her personally now that the response portion of the meeting is over.*] I have a question. I know you're not done, so like . . . from what I'm seeing so far it seems like your **message** is to like be true to yourself and don't let outside pressures get to you. Because her job is pressuring her to do things she knows isn't right, but she is kind of dealing with it. Is that the message you are going for?
Jillian:	Originally, I just started off writing and it did whatever, and then it kind of . . . it just sort of developed into this. And so now that is what I think I want to do. I think I might do that and have her give it up.
Kristen:	Because if that is your **message,** I think the way you are writing it is really helping to develop that.

Much can be said about this brief but rich response group moment, but if we reflect again on the pair of quotes from Gee (2004) that open the chapter, clearly the response group and the language of the group became tools that allowed these students to act, talk, and see themselves as writers. Jillian's unfinished work was taken seriously by Amanda, Dylan, and Kristen, who pushed to find specific lines in the text to support their reading and understanding of what the author was doing. They listened to Jillian's reading, making notes on the text that indicated places for comments. And they referenced these spots when they named and explained meanings and inferences they were making as first-time readers. Equally noteworthy, as the group members listened to one another, they added on to or extended an observation. As we listened, it seemed as though the members were benefiting and deepening their reading as they listened to one another. The boldfaced writerly language in Figure 4.6 illustrates the decisions students independently identify and use to make sense of how Jillian crafts her text and develops her purpose. The group provides an opportunity for students to use and apply language and academic concepts as writers in an authentic encounter with other writers.

Response groups also have a predictable ending. Generally, writers thank the group. They do not defend their writing or explain what the readers didn't understand. Some writers acknowledge a comment that helped them see their writing from a reader's point of view. Or they ask a question to clarify a comment. Jillian, who listened and took notes during the conversation, paused before she spoke, and Kristen asked a question about her intended message. Kristen seems invested in and curious about the future directions of the text and asks a genuine question based on her reading of it. And when Jillian honestly explains that she was writing forward without really planning a meaning, the question prompts a possible ending in Jillian's mind even though she seems to be trying to let the writing find its own way to an ending. Kristen ends Jillian's turn with a final comment. She does not tell her what to do. Instead, she takes the opportunity to compliment Jillian on a possible meaning her writing seems to be developing.

The influence of the group on the writer's identity and the writing may not be visible in this transcript, but each writer in this second writer response group session prefaced his or her reading with a summary of the changes he or she had made between this group's meeting and the last one. For example, Dylan stated that based on feedback from the group, he had redrafted two or three times the sections of his screenplay he had read previously. He added more details, following up on Jillian's fascination with his description of the quaint setting of the screenplay and Kristen's appreciation for the pacing of the opening. He also created two versions of a current ending, hoping to listen to the reactions of the group before he finalized the plot. It seemed clear that the response group initiated thinking and revisions for the writers even when no one left with a list of things that "should" be fixed or clarified. Both Jillian and Kristen noted in post-group reflective writes that shifting their comments from fixing the writing to noticing what the author was doing in the piece seemed more helpful to the writer. They further noted that it also seemed more helpful to the reader, who could focus more on what the writer was actually doing and what meanings that might suggest.

Let's return to the continuum of disciplinary literacy learning. Figure 4.7 summarizes the roles, actions, and disciplinary talk that illustrate learning that occurs in both the Project-Based and the Authentic sections of the continuum.

Figure 4.7. Disciplinary social practices.

	Developing Disciplinary Social Practices
Product or Performance	Engage in writer response groups several times during the process of drafting and revising a text written for publication beyond school.
Individual or Collaborative Performance	Develop routine ways of talking and engaging as a writer with other writers in a writer response group, adopting the social practices of a response group protocol.
Knowledge Development	Develop and apply knowledge of a genre: short fiction, poetry, memoir, and/or screenplay. Apply habits and strategies to develop a recursive writing process.
Expertise Development	Adopt the role of writer and critical friend in a writing community. Develop, retrieve, and apply a repertoire of habits, strategies, and processes to write and read that can be transferred to another text and/or genre.
Role of Teacher	Serve as coach and/or thinking partner in a community of writers as student writers engage in writer response groups.

Collegial Conversations: Who talks? What kinds of conversations do students have with one another or with you? In what ways do doers of your discipline talk to colleagues?

Find a friend or colleague to join you in the study of classroom routines and ways of talking to and with students.

1. Identify a lesson series or a project that your students will encounter during this school year.

   - In what ways do students talk as they engage with ideas, habits, and processes to develop a product, gain knowledge, or use expertise?

   - How might you redesign the lesson series or project to increase student talk or develop substantive conversations using disciplinary habits?

   - Consider activities that require students to talk in order to solve a problem or develop alternative views.

2. Invite a colleague into your room to observe ways you are incorporating talk or to study a disciplinary talk routine you are trying. Or visit a colleague's classroom to study the ways talk is used to support learning. Approach these early observations as open inquiries. Ask genuine questions that you might have about talk in your classroom, such as:

   - Who does most of the talking?

   - What kinds of questions do I ask? Who is answering those questions?

   - How many students talk during the hour?

   - How would I name and describe the ways I talk to and with students?

   - What protocols or strategies am I teaching to increase substantive conversations?

Engaging in Formative Assessment along the Way

"Kidwatching" can be described as (1) taking note of what students know and can do, (2) attempting to understand students' ways of constructing and expressing knowledge, and (3) using what is learned to shape curriculum and instruction.
— Gretchen Owocki and Yetta Goodman, *Kidwatching*

We hope that at this point in your reading, you are starting to think about how you might promote authentic literacy teaching and learning in your classroom and school. We also hope that you understand and accept that shifting from "doing school" to "doing the discipline" takes time and that there are various stages of change that can emerge in the adjustment of a task within a unit or in the design of a unit. And so we hope you are imagining some ways that you might engage students through expert performance, disciplinary lenses, and disciplinary talk. Still, if you're like us, one additional challenge arises: how to assess this kind of work.

As committed practitioners of "kidwatching" and formative assessment, we've learned through our work with the teachers you've met so far in this book how those approaches to assessment come to life in these classrooms that are focused on creating authentic literacy learning as described in the continuum of disciplinary literacy learning.

Early in our teaching careers, we worked with students who struggled with reading, writing, and content learning. These high school and college students often showed evidence of omissions and missing pieces in their learning. At that time, we were influenced by Owocki and Goodman's term *kidwatching*, which was more frequently employed in elementary school contexts. Today, we still value its communication of the holistic nature and spirit of what excellent teachers do, beyond what the more technical term, *formative assessment*, implies. But whatever we call it, when teachers are engaged in meaningful work that changes learning opportunities for youth, they are using formative assessment and engaging in kidwatching.

Entering classrooms from this place, we found it essential to carefully listen, observe, and talk about the strategies students used as they read, composed writing, and engaged in inquiry. Identifying both strengths and misconceptions allowed us to see the patterns in students' thinking and determine a next step to change habits these students had been ineffectively engaging in for years. As students enacted these next-step strategies, their interaction with writing or reading and understanding texts and concepts allowed us to see their thinking and evolving understandings. This work pointed us one step beyond kidwatching. What we learned is that it seems vitally important that students also watch themselves and their learning. And we are not alone in understanding this expanded way of thinking as part of well-planned, interactive formative assessment.

Black and Wiliam (1998) complicate the idea of formative assessment, suggesting that teachers who engage in daily formative assessment make the biggest gains:

> We use the general term *assessment* to refer to all those activities undertaken by teachers—and by their students in assessing themselves—that provide information to be used as feedback to modify teaching and learning activities. Such assessment becomes *formative assessment* when the evidence is actually used to adapt the teaching to meet student needs. (p. 140)

Faced with the call for daily formative assessment, we conclude that even helpful information drawn from summative assessments about the learning and the learner may come too late (Black & Wiliam, 2004; Popham, 2008; National Research Council, 2000). Other researchers suggest that daily communication in which students talk about their evolving understanding with the teacher in one-to-one conversations and/or with peers in one-to-one and small-group conversations need to be built into the instructional plan (Black & William, 1998; Popham, 2008; Hattie, 2009). John Hattie reframes communication and feedback from synthesizing 134 meta-analyses on achievement:

> The mistake I was making was seeing feedback as something teachers provided to students—[teachers] typically did not, although they made claims they did it all the time, and most of the feedback [teachers] did provide was social and behavioral. It was only when I discovered that feedback was most powerful when it was from the student to the teacher that I started to understand it better. When teachers seek, or at least are open to, feedback from students as to what students know, what they understand, and where they make errors, when they have misconceptions, when they are not engaged—then teaching and learning can be synchronized and powerful. Feedback to teachers helps make learning visible. (p. 173)

Designing open-ended activities that make disciplinary thinking and learning visible provides opportunities for teachers to learn from their students in order to adjust instruction daily and at the same time adjust student understanding of a discipline and disciplinary processes and knowledge.

Developing discipline-based formative assessment calls teachers to define the fundamental principles of the discipline and the difficulties students might have as they access prior learning to manage misconceptions and engage in inquiries that ask them to think through problems essential to doing disciplinary tasks (Black & Wiliam, 2004; National Research Council, 2000). Instruction connected to formative assessment for this purpose can potentially do the following: (1) aid teachers as they design instruction and learning progressions; (2) inform teachers as they adjust instruction to meet student needs; (3) develop partnerships with students as they engage in peer and self-assessment; and (4) develop student expertise and identities as experts as they work collaboratively on complex learning problems in a discipline (Black & Wiliam, 1998, 2004; Popham, 2008; National Research Council, 2000).

Daily Disciplinary Habits: Formative Assessment for Both Teachers and Students

Dick Moscovic and Duane Olds, Construction Trades
Oakland Schools Technical Campus Northwest

Partnerships: Local Network: Oakland Schools Technical Campuses; State Network: Michigan Construction Trades Association (MCTA); Regional Network: Oakland Writing Project (OWP); Community Partnerships: City of Auburn Hills–Hawkwoods Nature Center, The Well, Grace Centers of Hope, etc.

Formative assessment might be most tangible to both see and understand in carpentry. Carpenters know that everything that is built must be plumb, level, square, and flush. Everything a student builds can be assessed for these four characteristics of quality with just a few tools: a level, speed square, tape measure, and educated fingertips. Every carpenter carries these tools in his tool belt, and he pulls them out to confirm the accuracy of his work before he nails or glues anything in place. Equally important, these four concepts transfer from one construction field to another. Masons also carry the same or similar tools to ensure accurate and quality work. If students are building a house, they learn and transfer these self-assessment concepts and tools as they take the role of masons and lay the foundational blocks for a house; then students shift to the role of carpenter as they frame the house.

Errors matter, but errors are inevitable. A quality carpenter may have the mindset that creates quality workmanship, but she is also an expert at spotting and solving problems, and she knows that all problems have multiple solutions. Quality carpenters are flexible and creative thinkers. Even in new home construction, some errors can be visible to the eye or touch. Others may not appear until later in the construction of the house. There is a small margin of allowable error. If a foundation is off by a half-inch, that mistake is multiplied in each step that follows if it is not caught and repaired. The rough carpenter, drywaller, and trim carpenter all need assessment skills, habits that develop quality, and flexible thinking to identify solutions to any problem that already exists or that emerges during the work. Of course, *plumb*, *level*, *square*, and *flush* are everyday terms and they seem like common sense for anyone able to read a level, but they are difficult to achieve; and it is not easy for students to create a square wall even if they can read a blueprint and know the requirements to build a wall to code. All of this is why Dick Moscovic and Duane Olds teach students how to develop a mindset for quality work that eventually develops into a habit of formative assessment.

As teenagers, both Dick and Duane worked on construction crews. Their bosses taught them a basic process that transferred to almost any task and ensured quality: measure, cut, fit, and install. Today they teach their students that same process. Formative assessment is at the heart of this process. Student carpenters learn quickly to measure twice, cut long, fit, and cut a second time after the measurement has been confirmed. It takes only a few short cuts caused by incorrectly reading a measuring tape for students to understand the value of confirming and checking their work.

An example of this principle occurred during one observation at the 1920s house Dick's students were renovating. The exterior trimming crew measured a section of overhang on the house. They did not check the measurement. Instead, they cut a piece of fascia and then cut five more pieces the same size to save time. Fortunately, the team leader stopped them before they cut more pieces of fascia. The initial error caused the first piece of fascia to be cut short, so the next four pieces of fascia were cut short—some shorter than others. The error offered an opportunity for two lessons: (1) the value of self-assessment and (2) the importance of a process that builds a self-assessment habit into daily work practices.

First, Dick asked the students to identify the problem and to explain how they had taken the measurement and when they discovered their error. They explained that they took a single measurement and precut the pieces of fascia. When they went to install the precut pieces, they discovered that the overhang width was inconsistent, and all the precut pieces were short. Next Dick reminded them of the basic habit necessary to build a shed: measure, cut, fit, and install. He explained that this habit, used by all tradespeople, reduces waste and is used whenever they are cutting two-by-fours, trim, or fascia. Tradespeople know there will be subtle differences in measurements throughout a house. This home, as an extreme case, had no standard measurements that enabled pieces to be precut and installed. As a result, students learned that they needed to slow down. Instead of expecting standard measurements, they must adopt the habit of checking before they cut anything and do the following: (1) measure accurately the first time; (2) cut long; (3) fit the piece and measure a second time, marking the exact dimensions on the piece; (4) recut the piece to fit the variations in width or length; and (5) install the piece. He closed the lesson by reminding them that tradespeople anticipate quality, so assessment is built into everything they install.

As teachers, we know that a strategy as simple as *check your work* is not easy to teach. But we are pretty sure we didn't think of it as a disciplinary habit until we watched Dick's students make error after error, resisting spending the small amount of extra time to measure several times before cutting the fascia. Onsite an error translates quickly into a pile of scrap. Bottom line—errors cost money. That pile punctuates the value of self-monitoring because the teacher cannot make every cut, and once a cut is made, it cannot be undone. Quality must become a way of working. Therefore, onsite formative assessment is not just for teachers. It is for the students themselves as they engage in daily disciplinary tasks.

Let's pause to return to the continuum of disciplinary literacy learning. The instruction and enactment of formative assessment portrays elements from authentic learning described in the Authentic section of the continuum. A review of the series of decisions Dick made to create an authentic community of practice also reveals how he put into play a culture that develops disciplinary self-assessment habits (see Figure 5.1).

Figure 5.1. Teacher and student use of formative assessment.

	Authentic Work: Teacher and Student Use of Formative Assessment
Product or Performance	Students renovate a 1920s house that is in extreme disrepair for Grace Centers of Hope. Their task is to update the construction standards and meet city code. The project begins in February and ends in June.
Individual or Collaborative Performance	Students work in teams with team leaders. Highly skilled students manage more complex tasks independently or highly skilled students mentor other students as they complete a more complex task such as designing and installing a new support structure for the roof inside the attic or siding the front porch.
Knowledge Development	Students collaborate to gain multiple and competing perspectives on a task before and during construction.
Expertise Development	Students evaluate and reevaluate their knowledge as they encounter 1920s construction techniques that do not fit conventional twenty-first-century construction. They apply foundational knowledge and innovate new thinking as they test their work and develop a system for handling other similar problems.
Role of Teacher	Students work in teams in various areas of the house. The teacher designs the construction pathways to focus the construction and keep it on schedule. He moves through areas of the house to model skills and decisions and/or engage in individual conversations.

What Can We Learn from a Construction Classroom?

If we take Dick and Duane's way of thinking about formative assessment to ensure quality construction into an English classroom, we imagine, first, that students need several strategies to develop the mindset for quality writing. Teachers also need space in their daily lessons to talk with students. And finally, daily lessons need to provide an authentic task that engages students in fundamental disciplinary habits that can be applied in critical thinking, problem solving, and decision making.

Our question became this: what would we, as writers, substitute for plumb, level, square, and flush? What fundamental principles of writing could develop habits to assess movement toward quality work in the early stages of writing? These questions led us to create a commonsense list of characteristics that describe a writer's mindset for quality writing that we consciously use in our work as writers and that both teachers and students can see and assess:

- **Words on the page**—developing fluency, persistence, stamina, and a willingness to risk error and accept approximations
- **Minds on the page**—pushing to find something that seems new, interesting, or surprising; or pushing for a clarification that makes sense of complex thinking; or exploring a thought or argument to arrive at a new claim

- **Close observation of the world**—zeroing in on details; images; concrete, specific language; facts; examples; and information to describe what exists in the world and to push for multiple perspectives to expand our views

- **Flexible and creative thinking**—accepting that rereading, rewriting, abandoning, and rethinking are essential tools that provide opportunities to expand ideas

If this list framed formative assessment in writing classrooms, both teachers and students would focus their assessment on the decisions and developing identity of the writer rather than on the correctness of the writing. Teachers would no longer fix the writing in conferences with students. Instead, they would discuss a writer's planning decisions and the writer's view of the progress being made as well as multiple solutions to connect the writing to a reader and develop the meaning of the piece of writing.

Daily Formative Assessment: Shifting the Teacher Role in One-to-One Conferences

Carissa Peterson, Peter Haun, and Katie Locano, English Department
Oak Park High School

Partnerships: State Network: School Improvement Grant (SIG); Regional Network: Oakland Writing Project (OWP); National Network: Elevating and Celebrating Effective Teachers and Teaching (ECET2) Colleague Circles—Gates Foundation

Daily formative assessment, imagined as enabling students to make sense of the disciplinary strategies and processes modeled by the teacher, for us means working from the observations and research of John Hattie (2009, 2012). This sense making develops best when students engage in conversations with other students who are also making sense of the strategies and processes and in brief one-to-one or paired conferences with teachers who accept their role as coach rather than fixer of errors. This means teachers serve as expert-other but, more important, critical listener for strengths and misconceptions in order to name competencies and provide next steps. The design and planning for these daily conversations begins with the design of the unit, the series of lessons that support students as they create the unit's summative product or performance. And the summative product or performance moves students beyond reproduction of knowledge and into creation of knowledge. In an

English classroom, knowledge moves beyond the content of the reading and into knowing and applying the habits, strategies, and processes of "doers of the discipline." So students learn the strategies and processes of memoirists while writing memoirs. This disciplinary knowledge may be different when they move into writing argument and creating op-eds or writing informational texts. Each genre they study and write asks them to take on the role and habits of writers in that genre. In the end, students expand their understanding of the decisions writers use while creating a specific type of text or genre, develop their abilities to read these texts, and build expertise that can be retrieved and applied in future reading or writing.

To demonstrate what planned, interactive, daily formative assessment looks like in an English classroom, we visited Peter's room over the course of several days. At this point in the year, he was collaboratively working with Linda, Katie, Carissa, and Tatanisha Lewis, another colleague, to insert a pair of informational reading and writing units into their curriculum for the first time. The units focused on teaching a more authentic research process than they had previously taught, as well as providing a great deal of choice and decision making during the writing of the essays. The teaching and learning described in this classroom demonstrate Peter's commitment to positioning students as writers of a genre who are learning and applying the foundational habits of informational researchers and writers while conferring. Gaining understanding and the ability to apply and self-assess these habits became as important to Peter and the students as the unit's summative writing task. Together the team planned a lesson architecture that included a series of interactions each day that called attention to writerly habits as worthwhile knowledge and created a visible learning trail for both the teacher and the students.

1. Reflective Writing. Students began the hour with a five-minute metacognitive "Do Now" prompt that asked students to reflect on their expertise. Students answered questions like:

- What kinds of research projects have you done prior to this project? What do you like about research? What do you find challenging?

- How did collaborative research impact the evidence that you value, the various perspectives you have identified, and the research process?

- Describe how you managed the challenge of returning to the research one more time. You may or may not have found new information, but what did you gain from taking this additional research seriously?

- Has your informed view of your topic changed? If so, in what ways? How did organizing and connecting your evidence or your essay planning process impact the development of your informed view?

These metacognitive reflections provided a picture of each student's sense making. They also increased students' uptake of academic language.

2. Paired Rehearsal. Peter delivered a brief lesson in which he modeled a strategy or process that students would use that day or another day during the unit or future units. Then, as students tried out the strategy with a partner, Peter listened in on partnerships to identify ways students were making sense of the strategy, as well as their confusions or misconceptions. This gave him an opportunity to adjust and point out the effective ways students could apply the strategy before students moved into a thirty- to forty-minute independent workshop period.

3. One-to-One Conferring. Peter moved about his classroom, which was arranged in groupings of three student desks, translating to approximately ten groups of students. He made sure to stop at each group to confer with one student or pair of students each day. Although he conferred with a single student, he realized that other students were listening to the conference. Often the conference dealt with the same or similar decision that the other students in the group were grappling with. So a one-to-one conference often translated to a one-to-three conference. Peter often had time to return to a few individuals for a quick check on how the student had managed a next-step strategy.

4. Partner or Group Sharing and Feedback. During the last five minutes of the hour, students read aloud, discussed, explained planning and decisions, and provided feedback to their fellow writers.

Peter's collaborative work with both colleagues and students is an example of a teacher shifting into new formative assessment practices as he also transitions toward authentic work. Before we examine several one-to-one conferences, let's pause to look at the design of the work that includes elements from both Foundational and Project-Based sections of the continuum (see Figure 5.2).

We observed Peter as his students were in the early drafting stage of writing essays based on an inquiry question: what American rights are endangered? Before writing the essay, students read literature, informational and argumentative texts, and foundational United States documents and viewed seminal speeches by presidents and historical figures on the tensions between human rights and the common good. They used these texts to define the American character and social issues around human rights, and they studied the craft and structural decisions these writers used. Then students chose a right they believed was endangered and did primary and secondary research to develop an informed view and a stance on that view.

We then observed Peter after his students had spent two weeks in reading and research. His brief lesson focused on identifying and assessing information that illustrates a stance and informs a reader. Students used the hour to evaluate

Figure 5.2. One-to-one conferences.

	Foundational and Project-Based Instruction: One-to-One Conferences
Product or Performance	Are human rights established in the Bill of Rights endangered? After reading the Bill of Rights, other foundational US documents, and related readings, do collaborative research to examine this question and provide an informed response. Individually, write an essay that analyzes factors that protect or endanger human rights. What implications can you draw? Support your discussion with evidence from secondary and primary research.
Individual or Collaborative Performance	Students engage in daily peer conversations to discuss their thinking and gain feedback. Peter engages in 10–15 brief one-to-one conferences each day. Students interact in writer response groups several times throughout the unit as well as prior to revising and editing their essays.
Knowledge Development	As students plan and draft their essays, they develop strategies, reading and writing skills, and a process for sourcing, corroborating, and citing evidence that requires multiple returns to both secondary and primary research sources. This recursive research process helps students to develop an informed view of both engaging in additional research and writing an informational essay. They also discover what a self-assessment habit looks like and sounds like as they assess their words-on-the-page and minds-on-the-page habits.
Expertise Development	Students develop expertise in researching, analyzing, organizing, and synthesizing resources gained from collaborative and personal research. This recursive work enables them to learn and then retrieve and apply the strategies and processes of informational writers.
Role of Teacher	In daily interactions, Peter models, assesses, and adjusts student learning in the following ways: (1) he teaches a brief lesson in which he models a strategy or habit that students may use as they write; (2) he engages in one-to-one or paired conferences to gain insights into what students understand and are able to do to enact the strategy/habit in their writing; (3) he engages the student in a conversation to focus, adjust, or extend the student's current thinking, process, or work, and he provides a next step. When he walks away, continued assessment is in the hands of the students.

their essay plan, do additional research, and/or write a working draft of the essay. Peter spent the remainder of the hour conferencing with individual students. Each conference lasted two to four minutes. Both students and Peter were focused on assessing the essay draft in three ways: (1) Do I have sufficient information? (2) Do I have multiple sources? and (3) Do I have a variety of types of information? As we watched students writing, sorting through notes, and researching on their phones, we also listened to several conferences. Two conferences[4] illustrate the shift Peter and his students were making as they assessed the quality of their resources and created a working draft.

Mary's Conference (3 min. 56 sec.)

Mary was absent yesterday, but she had several paragraphs written. It was obvious that she had been working at home to catch up. Peter opened the conference by asking Mary what she planned to do today. Mary explained she had only one solid piece of research with her. However, as Peter glanced through her work, he could see that the single article was filled with evidence and that Mary's writing was specific and organized. This transcript is a small excerpt from the end of the conference:

Peter: So what have you decided to do?

Mary: Well, basically, I'm only using this one article because that is all I have right now.

Peter: So this one article. And you've been able to find all this information so far.

Mary: Yes. But I have a hard time getting started. I can't get a paragraph started.

Peter: You wrote all this from one article?

Mary: Yes.

Peter: You have a hard time getting started? So do you know what your position is?

Mary: Yeah, I wrote it down but it isn't right.

Peter: [*Scans several paragraphs Mary has written.*] So that's just in general, not just this essay? So you have a hard time writing the beginning of paragraphs?

Mary: All the time. I don't know what I'm saying. I just write stuff down. For the claim, I don't know if it is going to work with the other evidence I have.

Peter: [*Pauses.*] That's okay, Mary. What we're calling this is a working claim or position, which means it can be tweaked. If it is okay to use a word like *tweaked*. If you can get your idea down, then it can be changed around later. So long as you have some basic idea about what you want to say, you can use it as a guide to decide to research some more or change the writing around. Eventually, your writing should have most of the information laid out like you had hoped, but then you might need to go back and revise or edit or add.

Mary: Oh, Okay. [*Nods.*]

Peter: Okay, Mary. So between now and Friday, can you get more research and get your ideas on paper?

Mary: Right. [*Nods.*]

In this conference, Peter repairs Mary's misconception that her work lacks quality because she has only one article and she has a difficult time writing the beginning of paragraphs. In reality, Mary has done more specific writing around an idea than some students who have pulled a single fact out of an article and written a whole paragraph that is a general summary of the problem. Mary has culled several key facts and an example from her single article. Peter chooses to focus on building Mary's identity as a writer. He reminds her that a first draft is rough, and this first claim is called a "working claim," and she will have time to "tweak" it. He removes her worry about being confused or wrong by explaining the expectation that writers know they will change the early drafts of an essay. The conference freed Mary to continue writing with less worry. He also sends her off to do additional research so she can have the fuller planned draft that she had hoped to write. When Mary arrives in class on Friday, she will have a complete working draft with additional research. Getting her words and thinking on the page is the most important first goal for Mary.

Demond's Pair of Conferences (Conference 1: 1 min. 26 sec.; Conference 2: 1 min. 36 sec.)

In the first conference, Peter talked with Demond immediately after the lesson. When Peter arrived at his desk, Demond had several pages drafted in his notebook. Demond stated that he did not have enough facts to illustrate his point that the Second Amendment allows people to have guns to protect themselves but not to kill people. He decided to do research on his phone to find facts that would explain the difference between guns that are used for protection and guns that are used to kill. The following transcript captures a significant conversation during the second conference. In this conference, Demond reports on the focus of his phone research. He had successfully found facts, and the research provided both statistics and specific language (e.g., *AK family assault weapons*). Peter asks a question to confirm the effective research work and also emphasize the simple but explicit language that Demond might use to talk about his evidence and research.

> **Peter:** So when I left, you thought you needed more evidence and you were going to look up how many people were killed by guns.
>
> **Demond:** Which guns killed the most people.
>
> **Peter:** So did you find anything?
>
> **Demond:** Basically, this one article says that automatic weapons, AK family assault weapons, kill the most people.
>
> **Peter:** Oh, so you found that information. Who said that? Was it an authority?
>
> **Demond:** No. I don't think it said who said it. Just stated in the article.
>
> **Peter:** So it is a fact. You found that fact, and that was a really good fact because what you are saying is that you should be able to have guns to protect yourself but you don't need one of those kinds of guns. So gun for home protection is to stop but not kill someone.
>
> **Demond:** Right. There's a difference.
>
> **Peter:** Yeah. There's a difference. So that's a good fact for your claim.

Peter's approach in the two brief paired conferences provides support and gives Demond ownership of the work. Peter has found that if he stops to check on Demond (and other students like him) early, he can always count on Demond to use the modeled lesson and follow-up conference to set a goal. This goal setting enables him to try new things or extend his thinking, reading, or writing. In the first conference, Demond uses the day's lesson to assess his writing, name a clear goal to focus his independent work, and achieve it. The return conference provides a confirmation moment that builds Demond's confidence and sense of identity.

In these brief conferences, Peter takes the position of coach and sometimes modeler of thinking. He is respectful of the stage of the writing and encourages students to put their best thinking and writing on the page. Because Peter engages in daily conferences around his room, he knows the reality of student work and the daily growth that is occurring. Therefore, he involves students in a series of conferences to help them gradually take ownership of their writing, self-assess, and make decisions about developing and revising their writing.

What did Peter learn from all of the conferences? First, he discovered that many students had facts, but they lacked other types of information and resources that might require them to do additional research. He also noticed that the information in the drafts was general, and some students were telling personal stories rather than using information drawn from research. As a result, he generated a midworkshop lesson using student work as a model for finding authorities and inserting the words of these authorities into a text. He also collected writing samples from Demond and another student to write the next day's lesson on assessing and revising a first draft for two key qualities: focus and idea development.

Formative Assessment in the Midst of a Lesson: Developing a Personal Standard

James Tuttle, Bob Moses, and Greg Budzban

Partnerships:
Local: Ypsilanti Public Schools; National Network: Algebra Project; University Partners: University of Michigan Secondary Mathematics Lab and Southern Illinois University

Highly skilled teachers of various disciplines can construct learning opportunities that make students' levels of engagement, understandings of content, collaborative skills, and individual skill levels visible. Well-constructed lessons and activities can become important occasions for formative assessment, as well as powerful learning experiences for the students as they enact the lesson. But while student understanding is visible and observable by the teacher, often the assessment function is virtually invisible to the learner. However, teachers can respond to students based on the ongoing assessment information gathered in the midst of the lesson. The seamlessness of assessment and learning might be a goal we can all continually strive for. Before we describe and examine a carefully prepared lesson that embeds formative assessment through the concept of a decision tree, let's look at the design of the work, which includes elements from both the Foundational and the Project-Based sections of the continuum (see Figure 5.3).

Near the end of a two-week summer mathematics program with rising ninth graders, Bob Moses engages the struggling students in an activity that involves everyone in rehearsing mathematical discourse at some level but that also provides openings for the instructor to assess, in a formative way, individuals' functioning within a group or team. By organizing students to individually step up, select a number, walk the number through a decision tree taped on the classroom carpet, categorize that number, and, finally, offer an explanation to the class, Moses has created a venue for unobtrusively observing students' strengths and struggles. As individual students walk their factored numbers through the decision tree, they are demonstrating their understandings of prime factorization, their levels of self-confidence in mathematics, and their abilities to give a clear mathematical explanation. The use of a decision tree to categorize factored numbers is, of course, strategic: Moses knows full well that decision trees are used in everything from engineering to medicine to psychology. He envisions a day when students will encounter a decision tree in another context and have a memory of this activity and, perhaps, an idea of the ways decision trees function.

Figure 5.3. Assessing in the midst of the lesson.

	Foundational and Project-Based Instruction: Assessing in the Midst of the Lesson
Product or Performance	Students express their learning by using a decision tree as a tool to see emerging patterns in prime factorization. [In the world of work, mathematicians, engineers, economists, and doctors might use this tool to identify consequences in decision analysis.]
Individual or Collaborative Performance	Individual students walk specific numbers through the decision tree and provide brief explanations about their decisions. As the individuals are walking through the decision tree, small groups are responsible for a choral question or response.
Knowledge Development	Students learn two mathematical practices from the Common Core State Standards: (1) look for and make use of a pattern or structure and (2) look for and express regularity and repeated reasoning.
Expertise Development	The activity provides a first exposure to a decision tree. Students develop expertise in categorizing numerical patterns.
Role of Teacher	Bob Moses serves as a coach. He models how students will walk through the decision tree and how the chorus will question and respond. He listens critically during the process to watch for student confidence and understanding. He also presses students to explain their thinking.

Everybody in class, working in small teams over the two weeks, is given choral reading tasks. In small groups, they practice reading in chorus the following assigned statements:

Group 1: Do any of the prime factors of your number repeat?

Group 2: How many prime factors are in your number? Is the number of prime factors even or odd?

Group 3: Your number goes in the set of red numbers.

Group 4: Your number goes in the set of blue numbers.

Group 5: Your number goes in the set of yellow numbers.

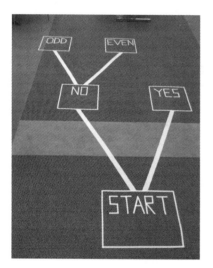

Bob visits each group, coaching them to speak out and to read in unison the assigned language. After a first feeble attempt at choral reading, he tells a group, "That doesn't do it. We're going to practice it until we get it right." They try again, counting to three, successfully reading in unison.

On the whiteboard, Bob has placed three color-coded charts with these headings: "Members of the Set of Yellow Numbers," "Members of the Set of Blue Numbers," and "Members of the Set of Red Numbers." He has generated a stack of cards with large numbers and their prime factorizations on them, taping the cards to a separate board. For instance, a card might read $210 = 2 \cdot 3 \cdot 5 \cdot 7$. Bob tells students they will be walking numbers through the decision tree that is taped to the carpet and then takes a card from the board, stepping onto the START square. He says, "I'll go first," and dramatizes the process, nudging each group to read their questions

as he steps on the appropriate squares. He has selected a card that reads $100 = 2 \cdot 2 \cdot 5 \cdot 5 = 2^2 \cdot 5^2$.

He tells them, "We've got to get you guys to read your questions together so everybody can hear them."

The first group says, "Do any of the prime factors of your number repeat?"

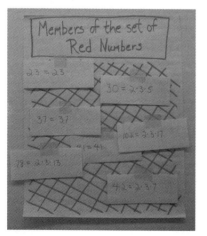

Bob says, "Yes," and pauses. "The person who is up here answers the question. I say 'yes,'" and then he steps onto the square labeled YES.

"And so I go to YES." The next group of students says in unison, "Your number goes into the set of yellow numbers."

Bob says, "It's a yellow number. Why is it a yellow number? Because the prime factors repeat."

Students take turns walking numbers through the decision tree until they make it through the entire stack of cards. Through this activity, it becomes evident who is feeling uncertain about the task, who feels confident about his or her understanding of prime numbers and factorization, and who has special strengths in offering clear explanations.

Bob's interactions with the students are firm but caring; they understand he is holding them to a standard. As individuals place their number cards on the appropriate charts, he presses for explanations:

> **Bob:**   Bryan, tell us why your number goes into the set of red numbers.
>
> **Bryan:**   Because it has an odd number of prime factors. [*Maurice walks a number through.*]
>
> **Bob:**   [*to Maurice*] "Why is 91 a blue number?"
>
> **Maurice:**   Because it's, they're, even.
>
> **Bob:**   Because what is even?
>
> **Maurice:**   The factors are even.
>
> **Bob:**   Seven is even? Thirteen is even? What is even?
>
> **Another student:** The *number* of prime numbers is even.

Bob then asks a student who has missed the introduction of the activity, "You want to take a number, Juan? Why don't you watch a couple more times until you're sure." After another student walks a number through the decision tree, Bob follows up with Juan, tracking to see whether he grasps what students are doing: "Juan, do you understand the questions?"

"Not yet," he says.

Another student, Sharon, tries walking a number through the decision tree. Her card reads $51 = 3 \cdot 17$. As she steps onto the taped square labeled "odd," a small group announces, "Your number goes in the set of red numbers."

"Caleb, why is 78 a red number?"

"There is an odd number of prime factors."

"I think I got this down," says Juan, as he steps up to walk a number through the tree, picking a card. As Juan walks through the taped decision path, fellow students pitch in and call out the answers to the choral questions. At the board, Juan triumphantly tapes the card to the blue chart. The group jointly constructs the explanation: "Eighty-seven is a blue number because it has an even number of prime factors."

By first inviting Juan to observe the decision tree activity and then checking in with him, giving him permission to decide when he is ready to "risk" demonstrating his thinking, Bob positions the student to self-assess. His interactions with Juan are observed by at least some of the other students, who then can see that it is possible in this classroom to decide for themselves whether or not they grasp an idea.

The decision tree activity of categorizing numbers into sets based on prime factorization puts students into the position of rehearsing mathematical discourse in a setting where they are slightly on the spot but also supported to take risks. The entire class is cooperating as coordinated subteams, so if they fail to read their piece accurately and in chorus, they slow the whole operation down. Bob, or any other instructor, could easily make brief observational notes, or use a checklist to determine individual or collective areas that need additional work.[5]

As the summer math program example demonstrates, teachers need to understand both the disciplinary literacies and the ways students think and act. Well-designed lessons allow teachers to observe and assess student understanding, providing information that allows them to shift instruction to respond to individual students. John Hattie (2012) states that lesson planning begins "with a deep understanding of what each student already knows and can do" (p. 42). Understanding the different ways students think, understanding the cognitive demands of the lesson, ensuring that students can engage in the thinking to enact the lesson, and assessing the minute-by-minute responses of students are all essential to advance the strategies students use to think and construct knowledge (Hattie, 2012; Shayer, 2003). Planning, designing, and instructing authentic tasks that respond to the ways students think call teachers to consider the role of kidwatching and formative assessment of student thinking in their daily interactions with students. Making this thinking visible is at the center of instruction design that creates opportunities for (1) classroom conversations that honor and encourage multiple and alternative views and the processing students use to arrive at those views; (2) one-to-one or small-group conferences focused on listening to student thinking; (3) kidwatching and observation of student thinking in the midst of instruction; (4) eavesdropping on student talk in partnerships; (5) observing in-the-moment writing or acting as students construct knowledge or a product; and (6) naming trends in brief reflective or metacognitive writes (Hattie, 2012).

Collegial Conversations: How might you shift to kidwatching and formative assessment?

With a colleague in your department, select a question or activity to explore your beliefs about assessment.

1. Reread one of the classroom examples in this chapter to label the actions of the teacher and students. Discuss how the ways in which teachers and students interact provide information that impacts student learning.

2. How did your view of formative assessment change after reading the chapter? How will this influence your formative assessment practices and lesson design?

3. Identify a lesson series that constructs knowledge across several days of instruction. Interrogate the lesson series to shift to daily kidwatching and formative assessment practices.

   - How are you currently assessing students?

   - In what ways are you gathering information to respond to individuals, gain a perspective on essential moves or thinking, or adjust your teaching? In what ways might you add practices to gather information about student learning?

   - How might you redesign the lesson series and activities so that daily learning

     ◦ becomes visible for both you and your students;

     ◦ provides opportunities for students to give you or their peers feedback in order to make sense and clarify their learning; and

     ◦ provides opportunities for you to observe and listen to your students to identify the range of understanding and trends in uptake of disciplinary language and concepts?

   - How might you examine student work and create conversations around student work so that students can develop self-assessment skills typical of disciplinary expertise?

Chapter Six

Partnering for Learning

Memories are more important than experience. Collaboration and partnership are best when together we acknowledge we are social beings who share stories.

  —Peter Shaheen, co-director, Oakland Writing Project

Peter Shaheen, Department of English
Seaholm High School

Partnerships: Local Network: Birmingham Education Association for Meaningful School Reform and Visual Learning Conference; Regional Network: Oakland Writing Project (OWP), Tech Smith PPP, and Drawbridge PPP; State Network: National Writing Projects of Michigan (NWPM); National Network: National Writing Project (NWP); Institute for Innovation in Education

Peter Shaheen, one of the most skilled collaborators we know, has chosen again and again to partner—in small and in large ways. His story, much as our own, teaches us: don't go it alone. An experienced high school English teacher, Peter has partnered with fellow forensics coaches; university faculty in English, teacher education, and information technology; elementary classroom teachers; and community leaders in projects such as *Making American Literatures in High School and College* (Gere & Shaheen, 2001), ImagineNation Matters (http://ics.soe.umich .edu/main/section/17), and Design Writing (Williamson, 2003). We've all learned it is important to find friends and partners on the inevitable journey to improve teaching practice, especially when pursuing disciplinary or cross-disciplinary depth. Learning to teach with effectiveness and impact in rapidly changing contexts is complicated, and it is necessary and ultimately rewarding to look for friends and colleagues who can journey with you. Another pair of eyes on a student project can help you improve plans and feedback. A detailed narrative of a curricular unit conducted in another state can spark you and your teaching partner to imagine new plans. Participation in an ambitious project involving community members, parents, and local university–based scientists can cause all concerned to think differently about learning, environmental science, and educational possibilities. Collaborating and partnering are so necessary to good work in education that the National Board for Professional Teaching Standards includes "Teachers are members of learning communities" as a key proposition of accomplished teaching.

Over time, we've noticed that the kinds of partnering teachers engage in can take many forms. In the examples that follow, we illustrate how teachers we've worked with have participated in partnership projects that fall into all of the categories listed in Figure 6.1. When Peter Shaheen began on the partnering journey, he began small, collaborating with a fellow teacher over a forensics project in which students shared work and gave one another feedback. His fellow teacher suggested that they arrange students from the classes into pairs and then support them to form friendships, or at least temporary buddy relationships. As Peter notes, that extra twist made quite a difference and eventually began to shape his view of the overall educational enterprise. More than twenty years later, Peter wonders what would happen if we were to conceive of education as the building of social capital through friendships and networks. He has a point—which he would probably never have arrived at without being part of so many amazing partnerships and projects.

Depending on where you are teaching, the opportunities readily available, and the directions you are prepared to head in, you might start with a small, serendipitous effort that gets larger and more intentional over time. After many years in education, valuing the growth that comes from innovative new partnerships, we've experienced virtually every kind of partnership and now engage in multiple part-

Figure 6.1. Types of partnerships.

Type of Partnerships	Within discipline	Multidisciplinary
Friends, colleagues, parents, community organizations		
Team, department or school		
University partnership		
Regional network		
National network		
Book-based, course-based		
Online		
Community-based or problem-driven		

nerships at any one time. The energy and patience we have expended in maintaining collaborations and partnerships have been returned to us a hundredfold.

Here are a few examples of the journeys teachers we have worked with have taken to go deeper into authentic instruction:

Middle school English. In the early 1990s, Southfield, Michigan, teacher Kathleen Hayes-Parvin partnered with her colleague Laura Schiller to work on strengthening opportunities for her sixth-grade special education students in English language arts. After she and Laura attended a National Writing Project Invitational Summer Institute in her region, Kathleen eventually began to add new partners and audiences for their writing: parents, second-grade students, high school students, and University of Michigan (UM) undergraduates. For two weeks over several summers, Kathleen co-taught with an excellent NWP teacher-consultant from another school district: Kathleen Kryza. The situation—ungraded, with middle school students from multiple districts attending a writing camp—let both of them experiment with drama, writing, reading, and presentation in ways they could borrow from during the regular school year.

High school mathematics. When James Tuttle was in his second year of teaching, the associate superintendent of his district asked if he would like to become involved in the Algebra Project. James agreed, and then had a host of amazing, challenging learning experiences over the next four years: (1) he attended a two-week workshop in Chicago; (2) he attended weekly meetings with UM mathematicians and mathematics educators; (3) he hosted Bob Moses, the civil rights organizer and AP founder, on a visit to James's classroom; (4) he observed Dr. Moses teaching his students for two weeks one summer; (5) he was coached by professional development consultant and coach Bill Crombie every two weeks for one and a half years; (6) he hosted the local Young People's Project meetings in his classroom after school; and (7) he traveled to South Korea with math educators and teachers to present a paper at the 12th International Congress on Mathematical Education. For James the journey may have begun with reading *Radical Equations* (Moses & Cobb, 2001) and with a desire to improve his mathematics instruction, but it blossomed into a multifaceted ongoing engagement, involving teachers in New York City; Los Angeles; Eldorado, Illinois; and Mansfield, Ohio, as well as mathematicians, math educators, and college students in Michigan and across the country. Collaboration happened in the classroom, in professional development workshops, and at formal meetings and conferences, but also through emailing, conference calls, and Skyping.

High school science. After fifteen years of teaching in Detroit and Ypsilanti, Michigan, Hans Sowder, named 2010 Michigan Science Teacher of the Year, was invited by his school district to become part of a newly established New Tech High School. Some of the features of the local New Tech included one-to-one computing, problem-based learning, cross-disciplinary team-teaching, and teacher-designed curricula using the New Tech framework. So this experienced, expert teacher had an opportunity to reimagine the teaching of science in this new context, working closely with colleagues at the school, but also networking with colleagues across the nation. Several years later, he shifted positions and was hired by the University of Michigan College of Engineering as an academic program officer. Subsequently, as part of a large, multifaceted National Science Foundation grant aimed at improving the modeling of climate change across the Great Lakes, he worked with a pair of New Tech teachers from his old high school to design a climate change study from multiple perspectives for eleventh graders, enacting instruction with Ypsilanti students and teachers with help from university scientists and graduate students.

Starting Small

While it's true that over time experienced teachers grow into incredible collaborators with extended networks—local, regional, national, and international—it makes sense to start with what fits your context and questions: what is necessary and what is doable, given your time and energy and your access to useful disciplinary resources.

For instance, your partnership journey might begin with the purchase of an interesting professional text—something like Troy Hicks's *Crafting Digital Writing: Composing Tests across Media and Genres* (2013). Or maybe the community library is hosting an author visit by YA author Christopher Paul Curtis, and you work with the school librarian to encourage book clubs around some of his texts, figure out whether he could visit your classes, or encourage families to attend the event. Or maybe, looking at student work, you notice that a significant number of students are struggling to write informed, crafted argumentative essays in spite of your best attempts to teach argumentative writing.

Often conditions change and new problems and issues emerge. Your decision to move toward more active, discipline-oriented teaching and toward more student-selected projects may cause a whole ripple of new work: reading professional texts; reviewing video footage; generating new plans, activities, and task sheets. A decision by the school board to move to one-to-one computing at your middle school may leave the most competent, confident practitioners struggling to learn new techniques and develop new policies. A sudden decision by the legislature to defund all professional development and assessments connected to a particular standards project may require that district and school-based educators reconsider a host of plans and activities, reimagining new pathways to similar aims. Friends and partners may be nearby or far away: in the classroom next door, former colleagues from a professional preparation program, Twitter buddies from #edchat or #nerdybookclub, or project collaborators in a different state.

Moving from Friendships to Partnerships

Having teaching friends isn't quite the same as forming partnerships with the intention of improving student learning. But friendships can become partnerships. All it takes is shared intentions to open up teaching practice, to engage in problem posing, study, observation, and data gathering, for the sake of improving student learning. Stepping into partnerships can begin with doable steps:

Sharing student work. Find two or three student work samples from your class that puzzle you or surprise you in some way. Meet your friend for coffee and ask him or her to look at the samples with you. Wonder a bit out loud about what you're seeing. Leave enough silence that your friend has room to speak, asking a question or offering a possibility.

Arranging for cross visitation. Ask a colleague you admire— outside or inside of your department if you can arrange to observe him or her teaching. Check in with the administration to see if you can get someone to cover a class so you can observe. Make it possible for your colleague to observe you, too. Take notes. Share your observations.

Planning a collaborative mini-project or unit. Think small: let your friend's students be an appreciative audience for your students for part of one class period. Or slightly bigger: have your students engage in a written project, prepare your friend's students to provide feedback in pairs or trios, and then bring the two classes together. And then a next step: actually co-plan and teach a mini-project with your friend—within your discipline or across your two disciplines. Try to take advantage of the different strengths you bring in knowledge, experience, and disposition. Afterwards, sit down together with some samples of student work and reflect on what you're seeing and what you'd do next time—or whether it even makes sense to do this particular study again.

Potential Pitfalls in Collaboration

While we have come to greatly value partnering and collaboration, we have learned not to be naïve. There are predictable problems, especially when attempting to partner with people and initiatives we don't initially understand well.

Timing. For any group of busy professionals with active family lives, one of the issues that necessarily determines a decision to engage fully in a partnership or collaboration is that of timing. If you've just had twins and you know that every waking hour must be directed to their care, this may not be the moment to sign on for a long-term, unfolding partnership that will require you to travel to various states and conduct extensive research in your classroom, in addition to your regular responsibilities. Or if you've just gone through a wrenching divorce, you might not be in a state of mind to add lots of extra conference calls and meetings to an already demanding schedule. What could be fulfilling and growth producing at one time in your life can become draining and exhausting if your parents are aging, if you're battling a health crisis, and so on. So it is important to accurately assess your situation and weigh the pros and cons before leaping into a major collaborative partnership.

Energy and resources. While we recommend collaborative partnerships generally, it is important to understand that the people who engage in them need to have at least a small reservoir of extra energy, and possibly some funds for flexible use. If you are partnering with a university researcher, for example, you might be invited at the last minute to travel to campus in order to participate in a conference or speak in a class. These unexpected opportunities are only useful if they don't throw your budget into serious trouble or don't wear you out within an inch of your life. The danger in not assessing energy levels and resource availability is that you may begin to resent your partner. When you move into a resentful stance, you will be largely unable to benefit from the connection, and eventually things will fizzle.

Earned trust. Quality partnerships cause the partners to gain knowledge of each other's strengths, areas of struggle, expertise, and life stories. In that process, trust is earned over time. People begin to trust each other when they do what they promise to do—when they accomplish, individually and collectively, the agreed-upon tasks. If you as partner don't come through, if you fail to make agreed-upon deadlines and meetings, the partnership will begin to wobble. It's best to address a faltering partnering relationship head-on, discussing the issues and problems that have emerged, and then either come up with a workable plan or disband the partnership.

Usable learning. As people who have pursued various partnering arrangements, we've learned that a partnership is fulfilling and will have natural momentum if what is being learned has evident use and applicability. Say you have a chance to participate in a summer workshop involving performance poets, student writers, and other teachers, hosted by the local university. If you can arrange to pilot a unit study on performance poetry in your classroom next fall, you will be more invested in the learning opportunity. Sometimes opportunities for partnering come up—say, serving as a research intern in a university engineering laboratory—in which the potential payoff is there, but it may be well down the road. Make sure you co-construct a plan with your partners to deal with the on-the-ground obstacles and barriers to using what you learn in your classroom.

Three Stories of Multidisciplinary Projects Emerging from Partnership

Great Changes in the Great Lakes Project

Great Changes in the Great Lakes?	
Types of Partnerships	**Multidisciplinary**
Friends, colleagues, parents, community organizations	All—Parent support of field trips and public presentation
Team, department or school	Interdisciplinary team
University partnership	University of Michigan College of Engineering
Regional network	
National network	New Tech Network
Book-based, course-based	
Online	
Community-based or problem-driven	Effects of climate change on the Great Lakes

Recently, Marcy Sliwinski, a chemistry teacher, and Melanie Depray Learst, an English and social studies teacher, both at New Tech High School in Ypsilanti, Michigan, collaborated with Hans Sowder, former New Tech teacher turned academic program officer for the nearby University of Michigan College of Engineering, and his colleagues to enact a six-week study titled "Great Changes in the Great Lakes?" The unit involved Marcy's and Melanie's eleventh-grade students, and the team ended up shaping the project to explore various kinds of argumentation and evidence—a timely focus given the attention to the Common Core State Standards in Michigan and across the nation. The driving questions for the unit were: "What is climate change?"; "Is it having an effect on water quality in the Great Lakes?"; "Why should I care?"; and "What can be done about it?" A partnership with university colleagues engaged in the generation of new models of the Great Lakes watershed and climate change factors influencing ecosystem health helped provide resources for speakers and field trips. In addition, the university resources made it possible to organize a study involving multiple frames, texts, and data sets—probably beyond the resources readily available to most teachers. By engaging with a research team that was itself engaged in focusing multiple lenses on climate change, the school efforts were greatly enhanced, though also complicated by additional layers of complexity.

Students and their teachers rode on a research vessel with scientists to test the water quality in Lake Erie. They studied a variety of arguments and counter-arguments about climate change, and they examined a broad array of data. They also reflected on and analyzed claims by biologists, chemists, climate scientists, economists, public policymakers, and historians—some of whom visited the class—weighing evidence and learning to distinguish between various disciplinary lenses. At the end of the study, students presented their findings at a public event held on the university campus. Working in small teams, they created poster displays of their findings and took turns giving explanations to guests. Many posters included multiple categories, such as "an engineering perspective," "a chemistry perspective," and "a biology perspective," and students listed the kinds of information and evidence they had encountered that fit the specific lens. Students reported that the study made them recognize that the problem of climate change was actually having an impact on them and the world they were inheriting. While not every student decided to become a scientist, many students noted that they found the whole project important and interesting. The event was attended by university faculty, graduate students, school district personnel, and parents.

But just because a collaboration and partnering attempt ends up being memorable and extremely worthwhile doesn't mean it all flows smoothly without complications. In this particular case, Marcy and Melanie had been newly assigned into a school-based team different from the initial group that Hans Sowder had talked with to establish an agreement about the project. In fact, Marcy and Melanie were just getting to know each other as teaching partners. Inevitably, they relied on their college collaborators to arrange for visits by scientists and others partnering on the larger climate change and Great Lakes watershed project. Some of the visitors were unused to conversing with diverse high school students and weren't able to tailor their presentations to resonate as fully with student questions and interests as might have been ideal. Both Marcy and Melanie are now thinking about the kinds of supports and initial conversations teachers could have with community presenters so that classroom visits can be as useful as possible.

Additionally, Marcy's students were taking chemistry—and although this project involved lots of science, it didn't always aim squarely at chemistry outcomes. Marcy and Melanie have tons of ideas about ways they could improve the study if they had a second chance to enact it, but they probably won't have that opportunity, and certainly not in the exact same fashion—in fact, Melanie is being transferred to a district middle school next year. Still, Melanie says, "I learned a lot. English language arts doesn't have to be driven by narrative. I know this as a social studies teacher, but I really enjoyed getting the kids to write and speak from these various points of view."

Problems and Possibilities

The previous example begins to point to the struggle of collaboration: by their very natures, disciplines have specific knowledge bases and ways of working. On the one hand, it could be considered "efficient" to plunge someone into a particular discipline, to introduce a specialized vocabulary, and to focus on the key content outcomes. On the other hand, if Marcy had only aimed squarely at chemistry without opening up to the broader domain of scientific inquiry and to the various players and ways of arguing about climate change, her students might think of chemistry as merely a course. After the climate change study, they know that chemistry has a real role in the discussion, but it certainly isn't the only lens to use as we navigate the topic.

The project that Marcy, Melanie, and Hans developed holds promise for highlighting a common communications thread across disciplines, applied fields, and professions: the process of making an argument. Even if a teaching team or school doesn't have access to the resources around climate change that a university research connection can bring, the idea of introducing the different ways in which disciplines and fields make arguments about a particular topic is an idea worth developing into a project or unit. Argumentation is an important way that human beings engage with one another, making cases for certain preferred frameworks for understanding, approaches, and even artifacts and objects. Arguments are made everywhere, but the preferred evidence and structure of these arguments differ considerably. If we really dig into the different kinds of evidence and the varying structures, we can help students navigate diverse situations effectively, leveraging what they are learning in their various classes. When teachers are partnering with multiple disciplines, making the differences in argumentation and evidence visible also helps students understand how disciplines are different and asks them to think, read, write, and inquire in different ways. Figure 6.2 is a chart illustrating how arguments and evidence differ across disciplines and fields. The courage Marcy, Melanie, and Hans demonstrated in moving ahead to make something exciting and memorable happen for the Ypsilanti New Tech eleventh graders in the face of collaboration complexities gives them all a powerful experience that can lay a foundation for other collaborations and partnerships in their teaching futures.

Figure 6.2. Argumentation across disciplines.

	English Language Arts	**Mathematics**	**Science**	**Social Studies/ History**
What counts as evidence	Narrative and anecdote; quoted literary passage; material from all disciplinary frames	Empirical, verifiable observation, diagram, or calculation	Graphs, charts, statistics drawn from experiments, and empirical observation	Historical records: documents, photographs, and accounts, both primary and secondary
Important ideas	• Sequence • Different perspectives and points of view drawn from identity • Genre constraints and possibilities	• Everyday language to abstract symbolic representation • Multiple ways of representing a problem	• Developing models • Constructing explanations • Designing solutions • Structure and properties of matter • Chemical reactions • Patterns (Next Generation Science Standards, n.d.; National Research Council, 2012)	• Sourcing • Corroboration • Contextualization (Wineburg, 1991)

Doing Business in Birmingham Project

Doing Business in Birmingham	
Types of Partnerships	**Multidisciplinary**
Friends, colleagues, parents, community organizations	All—Parents as initial business collaborators
Team, department or school	Interdisciplinary team
University partnership	
Regional network	
National network	Microsoft Partners in Learning
Book-based, course-based	
Online	
Community-based or problem-driven	Sustainability in local business practices

For two middle school teachers, Rick Joseph and Pauline Roberts, partnerships became the driving force in their development of a "sciracy" project called Doing Business in Birmingham, a winning project in the 2012 Microsoft Partners in Learning US Forum. Sciracy blends science and literacy to enable students to learn science concepts and processes through participation in civic affairs. This project provided students with the opportunity to develop a wide range of literacies as they learned about sustainability and navigated a range of business and civic settings in their community.

Rick and Pauline began their journey into partnerships when they realized that they shared fifth- and sixth-grade students but really didn't know what was happening in each other's classroom. So they decided to create a project together that took them into partnership with their students. This kind of collaborative thinking started them on a journey to understand sciracy, to research sustainability and sustainable business practices, and, eventually, to create a green business rating system. Students worked in teams to educate themselves and others on the ultimate goal—sharing how sustainability can save money and support the environment.

The partnerships grew from there as students scripted cold calls by phone or in person to local businesses; created a sustainability checklist, interview plan, and brochures; and prepared a website. Finally, four-person teams made up of interviewers, photographers, videographers, and materials managers were formed. The teams were organized to educate others and to capture the historical record of the work that took them on field trips to 100 businesses in their local community. Students were greeted at some companies by sustainability officers, but most often the students met with the owner or manager of stores and businesses. Through the interview process, students enlisted companies to become partners in maintaining sustainable business practices and to earn Green Star ratings that would be reported on the class website. Students maintained a relationship with these companies across the year and provided companies earning Green Stars with decals for their front door or window. A company could earn a single Green Star for five sustainable business practices. As companies developed additional sustainable practices, they earned additional stars. If a company earned five Green Stars, they moved into the Gold Star category.

Rick and Pauline and their students from Coventry Middle school won first place in the Learning Beyond the School category at the Microsoft Partners in Learning US Forum in Seattle, in which 75 projects from around the country competed. They also won first place in the Collaboration category at the Microsoft in Education Global Forum in Prague, in which 150 projects from around the world competed. But, Rick explains, the most important moments of the project occurred as students developed critical thinking skills in a classroom setting and then used them in the real world. The students became agents of change in their own lives. Rick adds:

> If they feel empowered in this project, they can face fears and anxieties to make other changes occur. They can harness the synergy of collaborative work to gain confidence to develop a process that will enable them to take on complex problems in their lives and communities. These students became empowered to act instead of watch and to learn for learning's sake.

The project went beyond sciracy by engaging students in multiple disciplines to understand and act on a social problem. Students integrated

- **Mathematics** to analyze and aggregate data
- **Science** to understand sustainability, the impact of climate change, reduction in resource allocation and use and its impact on ecology and environment and habitat destruction, and the impact of human behavior on systems
- **Social studies** to understand the difference between wants and needs; resource allocation across countries and cultures; the imbalance and inequity in resources and allocation as a social question; the western European worldview; and the role politics plays in the environment and eventually in families. Students explored the question: how do we view the world, our role in the world, and the tension between public domain and privatization?

- **English** to demonstrate competency in five domains: listening, speaking, reading, writing, and thinking to inform in expository and persuasive writing and persuasion in speech
- **Digital technology** to create printed and visual and auditory media texts and products used in the world

In the end, the collaboration, multidisciplinary learning, and social roles as experts in authentic contexts gave Rick and Pauline's students a sense of power as they exceeded the typical position young people take with adults in professional settings. They engaged with business partners using professional language linguistically and academically beyond typical fifth and sixth graders.

Sunrayce World Solar Challenge

Sunrayce World Solar Challenge	
Types of Partnerships	**Multidisciplinary**
Friends, colleagues, parents, community organizations	All—Parents support fundraising and travel, Ironman Triathlon and Bank of America
Team, department or school	Interdisciplinary team
University partnership	
Regional network	
National network	Sunrayce
Book-based, course-based	
Online	
Community-based or problem-driven	Designing, building and racing a solar car

Sometimes a multifaceted partnership early in teaching can change a person's vision of what is possible in education, and ultimately affect the trajectory of a career. In 1992, Stephen Best was new to Konawaena High School in Kealakekua, Hawaii, his third school in as many years. He taught mathematics but was also certified in physical science and had a limited background in engineering from a high school internship experience and undergraduate coursework. During his second week, Stephen met Bill Woerner, the lone physics teacher, who mentioned a three-year-old extracurricular club centered on the design and creation of a solar-powered vehicle. Bill was in the process of designing a project-based learning academy for the school and invited Stephen to take on the solar car team with Bill's mentoring. The solar car team began as part of a statewide effort to encourage the use of solar energy as a viable energy source and as a way to engage youth in authentic learning. The culminating event, a state solar car race, had recently been discontinued, but the students wanted to sustain the team and to design and build a new solar car that could potentially compete in the Sunrayce, or the World Solar Challenge, the following year.

Funding was key. The two teachers and their student team brainstormed potential partnerships and identified sources of financial support. Unlike other projects, in which teachers and administrators often do the heavy lifting around proposal writing, the students themselves began developing funding proposals to initiate the work. Proposal writing was a core practice that would effectively make or break the team since the work could not go on otherwise. Participants from previous years began documenting the history of the project to date, pricing materials, and brainstorming potential funding sources or opportunities within the community.

Two early opportunities proved fruitful: the Ironman Triathlon, looking to expand its support to local groups, invited the team to participate in local fundraisers at the triathlon. In addition, Bank of America provided a substantial grant and, as part of a statewide advertising campaign, collaborated to create an ad featuring the team. These early partnerships not only provided the funding necessary to address the other goals, but they also introduced students to authentic cross-disciplinary project activities, including marketing, budget planning, and project management for media productions, including the TV commercial and the promotional booklets and brochures for the Ironman event. Students formed committees and identified tasks and roles for each, but they also invited other students from the team into these activities as reviewers, participants in the commercial, and other events.

Sometimes authentic work is not of a single disciplinary nature; ambitious projects often require a coordination and integration of multiple disciplinary tasks and roles. In this project, student expertise developed in two stages. Those tasked with an initial role, such as proposal development or marketing coordination, had the opportunity to learn from professionals in these fields from the sponsoring organizations' efforts. These individuals became leaders of these facets of work for the team and then involved others through "task committees" to engage in, and learn from, the work. Each task included both peer review and teacher review to ensure the work was complete and appropriate.

Work on the solar car design began in a similar fashion. The students worked with Stephen and Bill to come up with a structure for organizing design and construction of the car. They identified the major tasks of the design, such as the creation of the overall structure and look of the car itself; design of the frame; design of the solar panel and underlying electronics; design of the drivetrain; and design of the auxiliary functions such as steering, braking, access to electronics, and driver compartment. Students then used a "backwards design" process to identify time lines using the Sunrayce event, which was to take place the following summer in the continental United States, as the target goal so that all design and construction efforts took place beforehand. They recognized that they could not design the braking system for the car until they had decided on the type of electric motor they would use, what the frame design would be like, and how the steering mechanism would be designed. Placing all aspects of design and construction on a giant Gantt chart allowed everybody to see what needed to be done when, and what the task and outcomes of each committee would be. It also helped in designing the process for recruiting new students into the team during the year.

As design and construction got under way, Stephen worked with students to constantly reassign roles and learning functions. The team's goal of competing in the Sunrayce was upended when they were told that "only collegiate or professional teams could participate," but they simply adjusted their aims to say, "We are going to take the car to the mainland anyway, and while the Sunrayce traverses the Great Plains, we will become the first such team to travel coast to coast across North America." Although forty students worked on the team over the course of the year, there was only room and funding for a team of seven students, along with Stephen, Bill, and a parent, to travel to the mainland. Consequently, Stephen had to ensure that the team would include students capable of driving, handling repairs on any aspect of the car, handling logistics and media events, and dealing with critical other work. A sort of jigsaw learning effort had to take place to fill gaps in understanding among the smaller traveling group while also keeping others involved and engaged to complete the construction of the car.

As the new team director, Stephen did not—and could not—act as the "expert" who taught students the skills or components of a task. Rather, he took on the role of learner himself to better facilitate the work. This experience helped him move from viewing teaching traditionally, as "presenting and conveying information and skills in engaging ways," to viewing teaching as the facilitation of student-led, authentic learning. Stephen's teaching experience led him to want to know the details of each component of the work, which resulted in asking a wide variety of questions throughout each process of both the adult partners and the volunteers who were content experts in engineering, marketing, and logistics planning, and of the students who were leading these efforts. The more he modeled questioning early on, the more his students began asking a broader range of questions them-selves. Stephen's questioning of the details of student work on the project dimin-ished over time as students became more aware of the questions to ask and became clearer on the comprehensive descriptions they would need to proceed. Stephen summarizes this learning:

> As a novice, you don't know what you don't know, and sometimes you don't know how to ask the right questions, or have the confidence to do so. So, if you see some-one asking the questions and talking through the learning that is taking place, you, as a student, begin developing your own metacognitive skills to recognize what you are learning, how you are learning it, and what you need to learn. Sometimes, the best work a facilitator of authentic learning can do is to allow students to learn vicariously by modeling the learning process for them and making the connections to the learn-ing obvious by talking through them or demonstrating them with the task at hand.

This early experience with an incredible, multifaceted project involving a host of partners—other teachers, local businesses, parents, and the students themselves—clarified a vision of educational possibility and lit a passion within Stephen Best. Subsequently, he has designed and facilitated professional learning for teachers in mathematics and science at the state and national levels, and he is currently work-ing in the Michigan Department of Education to open new opportunities for youth and their teachers.

Your Road to Authentic Literacies

The road we have invited you to journey down—a road that leads to a more en-gaged, authentic disciplinary depth that results in student ownership and agency—is the kind of road we've been on over the course of our careers. Perhaps it makes obvious sense why we need to keep learning and growing as educators, but to be clear, we feel an urgency. Here's why.

More than 90 percent of American eighth graders and 80 percent of low-income eighth graders say "Yes!" when asked whether they intend to go to college. Yet a much smaller percentage actually ends up at a college campus, and a group that is smaller still makes it all the way through to college graduation. Our pipeline is incredibly leaky. If you maintain a "safe" distance from the lives and communi-ties most affected—the kind of distance too often kept by politicians, legislators, and pundits—this is a policy problem for the nation. But if you are a teacher, parent, or community member encountering young people whose dreams and future prospects have been dashed, you understand that this situation, this lack of investment in youth and their futures, is an ongoing heartbreak, with local, state, and national consequences. Lives are being wasted. There is a human cost, as well as a profound societal cost, when young people don't have access to learning that is useful, meaningful, and applicable in careers and citizenship. Together, we educators can take concrete action to move our practice on the continuum of disciplinary literacy learning. Let's partner purposefully. Let's do as the young education activist Nikhil Goyal asks: let's make the world their school.

Collegial Conversations: What partnerships might begin or extend your journey to authentic literacy in schools?

On your own or with a colleague or your department,

- Identify goals to get started or extend your work toward authentic literacies in your classroom or course. Consider small steps to get started or collaborative partners to stretch your thinking.

- Use the Types of Partnerships table (Figure 6.3) to identify current partnerships and explore new partnerships that might support you on your journey to literacies in your discipline.

Figure 6.3. Types of partnership reflection.

Type of Partnerships	Within discipline	Multidisciplinary
Friends, colleagues, parents, community organizations		
Team, department or school		
University partnership		
Regional network		
National network		
Book-based, course-based		
Online		
Community-based or problem-driven		

Appendix: Student Work Samples and Reflections

These self-selected genre drafts and reflective responses have been drawn from the student writing group featured in Chapter 4 on pages 76–79. First are multiple drafts and a reflection by Jillian, the student whose work was being discussed in the transcript. This work is followed by drafts and reflections written by Amanda, Dylan, and Kristen, the other members of the group. All of these students were seniors enrolled in Advanced Placement Literature at Clarkston High School in 2014.

JILLIAN: Draft 1—Response Group 1

March 20, 2006

Dear Diary,

I stand here looking at everyone else. They don't notice me or even bother to look up. They don't notice all the little flaws I see in myself. I see all theirs, every single one. They also don't understand how I know. They and everyone else in this world view me as perfection, but I don't. I don't see how all this exploitation is perfect, nothing about my life is perfect. I'm never in one place for very long and home, I never get to go home. In Paris, Madrid, London, and New York I feel like just another person roaming the streets and not what society labels me. I stop at little magazine stands and see so many people raving about the lifestyle of the rich and famous, little do they know that it's not that easy.

I'm jealous of the people I walk by that don't live in the spotlight. This huge spotlight follows you and reveals every single aspect of your life. All these people have no idea what the spotlight does to you. It destroys you, nothing is ever the same. Stepping into the spotlight means stepping into a world with nothing but lies and rumors. There's no going back, you're stuck there forever. There's absolutely nothing you can do for one little mistake. Whatever you do is plastered on tabloids, magazines, the internet and it's there forever. It changes you, you are forced to live in a world under a microscope. Those people looking at you through that microscope don't understand how hard it is to be you. They think being a model is living the dream but it's only a nightmare.

I can't do what they can do. I can't walk outside with no makeup on or my hair not done. I have to look like a poster child for basically everything. I don't understand why they call me perfect. I'm not perfect they just hide my imperfections. They know I wear makeup because that's how they always see me. I'm merely a mannequin for them to place clothes on. I walk the runways while they take photos of me in some ridiculous so-called "art" that I'm really not to fond of. I don't know why I do this and people praise me. This career is not all the glamour that they make it out to be. It is a full time job and more. This job can't replace all the things I've done to myself. I've been forced to do awful things. I'd go days without eating, only chewing on ice and going to the gym for hours on end. Maybe I'll just quit tomorrow. Who am I kidding they flew me to Paris, there's no way I'm quitting.

So long Diary

Jessica

JILLIAN: Draft 2—Response Group 2

August 20, 2006

Dear Diary,

I stand here looking at everyone else. They don't notice me or even bother to look up. They don't notice all the little flaws I see in myself. I see all theirs, every single one. They also don't understand how I know. They and everyone else in this world view me as perfection, but I don't. I don't see how all this exploitation is perfect, nothing about my life is perfect. I'm never in one place for very long and home, I never get to go home. In Paris, Madrid, London, and New York I feel like just another person roaming the streets and not what society labels me. I stop at little magazine stands and see so many people raving about the lifestyle of the rich and famous, little do they know that it's not that easy.

So long Diary,

Jessica

September 22, 2006

Dear Diary,

I'm jealous of the people I walk by that don't live in the spotlight. This huge spotlight follows you and reveal every single aspect of your life. All these people have no idea what the spotlight does to you. It destroys you, nothing is ever the same. Stepping into the spotlight means stepping into a world with nothing but lies and rumors. There's no going back, you're stuck there forever. There's absolutely nothing you can do for one little mistake. Whatever you do is plastered on tabloids, magazines, the internet and it's there forever. It changes you, you are forced to live in a world under a microscope. Those people looking at you through that microscope don't understand how hard it is to be you. They think being a model is living the dream but it's only a nightmare.

I can't do what they can do. I can't walk outside with no makeup on or my hair not done. I have to look like a poster child for basically everything. I don't understand why they call me perfect. I'm not perfect, they just hid my imperfections. They know I wear makeup because that's how they always see me. I'm merely a mannequin for them to place clothes on. I walk the runways while they take photos of me in some ridiculous so called "art", that I'm really not to fond of. I don't know why I do this and people praise me. This career is not all the glamour that they make it out to be. It is a full time job and more. This job can't replace all the things I've done to myself. I've been forced to do awful things. I'd go days without eating, only chewing on ice and going to the gym for hours on end. Maybe I'll just quit tomorrow. Who am I kidding they flew me to Paris, there's no way I'm quitting.

So long Diary

Jessica

September 3, 2006

Dear Diary,

I'm back in New York for fashion week. I loved Paris, but I'm so exhausted from work. I feel better now that I'm not surrounded by all that fattening French food. I swear anything that went down my throat went straight to my thunder thighs. But it's better now because I didn't eat one thing since I've been back, so I should be all set for next week. I may have to break down soon then head to the gym. I'm actually on set right now for a fitting and they told me I needed to lose an inch on my waist. That shouldn't be too hard, I've done it before. But lets keep that between us. . . .

So long Diary,

Jessica

September 6, 2006

Dear Diary,

I did it! 3 days of cold ice and pure sweat, there goes that silly little inch. Those designers thought I couldn't do it, well ha, I did! I'm so excited and worried and kind of scared . . . but that doesn't matter because it's the most wonderful time of the year!

I just saw my best friend on the cover of vogue magazine in the lobby today. Everyone said she looked absolutely perfect, which I completely agree. I could never look as good as her, why do you think I had to go to the gym for 3 hours yesterday? I'll admit it was worth it. Now all I have to do is stay this way for only a few more days. Empty is strong, empty is perfect. That's another secret you're going to keep too. I don't want anyone to know.

So long Diary,
Jessica

September 7, 2006

Dear Diary,

I'm sitting in a cozy chair at the empire coffee shop. I decided that after my second fitting today I could treat myself to a cup of coffee and a good book. Well this book really isn't that good because writing sounded like a better idea. I can't wait until tomorrow! I get to do what I do best, be a model. I will admit that getting up at 6am and working until 8pm will be a struggle. I know I'll make it through like I always do. My day will start out with rehearsal, then makeup, then hair, then final fittings, then the runway, and then the parties. But I live for this, so there's really no complaining. I always love seeing everyone's faces when we float onto the catwalk. They're looking at 2 works of art, and we're 1 of them. But my coffee cup is now empty unlike my stomach so it's time to leave this cozy chair and prepare for tomorrow.

So long Diary,
Jessica

September 9, 2006

Dear Diary,

Yesterday was the worst day of my life. Absolutely awful. No one will ever forget that day. I can't believe that happened. I'm putting all of my frustration into this and I don't know what to write. First, it's a little after midnight and I'm stuck in a hospital bed. Apparently I was "under nourished" yesterday when I was working. Come on, everyone knows that you don't eat the day of runway, you just can't. There's also too many needles stuck in my body that I just want to rip out. They're destroying me, I can feel it. There's nothing wrong with me, so I don't know why I'm here. I keep asking the nurses if I can leave and they say not until my levels are up. I don't care about my levels I want to escape from this place. I try to tell them that I'm not doing anything wrong. It's my job, everyone knows, and it's all their fault. I have to be thin to work, they made me this way. But they're moving me to another room downstairs, what ever that means. . . .

So long Diary,
Jessica

JILLIAN: Response Group Reflection

I felt when we discussed our works in the response group without the ability to make corrections we tried making more text-to-text connections. We had to form questions about some things that we were unsure of, and then were able to discuss them openly. We were able to think differently because we had to ask about the work from both a reader and a writer's perspective. After discussing with each other we were able to make more sense of the meaning behind the work because we each had differing thoughts on the pieces.

AMANDA: Draft 2—Response Group 2

My Priest told me during mass that faith is like the wind. You cannot see it, but you can feel it. He also said you cannot capture it in a box, that wind needs to remain moving and trying to box your faith will kill it. The cliché discussion almost made me vomit, but it made me think of how wrong he was. But of course, everyone else nodded in agreement. It's like dogs surround me, obeying everything their master says. I'm sorry, but I don't do that. Don't get me wrong, I love the idea of faith and the practices, but I can't get myself to fully partake. Also the idea of agreeing to someone without any thought is lost on me. Maybe it's because my mother is crazy and taught me to believe no one (yeah she has trust issues). Either way, I sat in the church bench, arms crossed and head bowed; pretending to pray when in reality I just stared at my paint splattered Nike's. I looked at the design, created from last's years mission trip and smiled at the thought. I had experienced faith going out and working in the blistering heat. My faith might not have been in a god, but it was definitely in people. How could the priest say you can't box up your faith, when I have my faith stored in memories? I snapped out of my thoughts as my mom yanked me out of my seat and threw a bible into my hands. Joy.

I lay in bed; my batman onesies covering my body and the sound of a crackling five-dollar Target candle filled the air. I would stay like this forever, avoiding social interaction and wearing awesome pajamas. However, every Saturday my dad insists I get out of bed so I don't "waste the day away." I'm not wasting my day; I'm just spending it my way. Never the less, like clockwork, I could hear his heavy footsteps come up the stairs. I quickly blew out the candle and pretended to sleep, awkwardly sprawling my body out among the sheets.

"Rachel, wake up!" My dad whispers, his voice loud in comparison to the quiet I experienced earlier. His always does that, whisper. I hate it. He could just speak normally. We could be home alone in the middle of the day, and he would still whisper. I don't understand this man.

"Dad, stop whispering. And it's Saturday. Just let me sleep," I groan, rolling over so I could bury my face in the pillow. The ceiling light clicked on, illuminating my room. I moaned again, and rolled on my side to glare at my father. His sweater vest and cowboy combination killed me, but he only smiled and left, keeping my door open so I was exposed to the noise from downstairs.

"Dang it." I mumbled. I rubbed my eyes and rolled off the bed and onto the floor, so I could crawl to the door.

The kitchen is always so bright in the morning, so I squint to make it to the fridge. My mom is sitting at the table cutting out coupons for Kroger, dead silent. I scrunch up my noise in confusion and narrow my eyes. Why are you acting so strange, woman? My inner gangster is coming out. It's too early for this. I pinch the bridge of my nose and open the door, searching the fridge for any edible content. My house is always stocked with food, hence the Kroger coupons, but that doesn't mean I like the food. I scanned over the fruit and lunchmeat and then the yogurts. Nope, nothing. I reclose the fridge and make my way to the coffeemaker.

I turn the machine on, the smell of coffee grounds immediately fill my nose. I lean on the counter, my back hitting the corner of the kitchen island. I decide to stare at my mom. There she goes, slipping away. I clear my throat and wait for her to turn around.

"Ahem," I say louder, my eyes growing large in impatience. I tap my fingers on the counter, my nails clank across the granite. I should really cut these bad boys, long nails are just scary.

"Yes, Rachel?" my mom asks, but really it was a statement. There is a hint of ice in her voice. Weird.

"Anything wrong Mom? You're off today," I answer honestly, seeing she's in mood to mess with. If she was, I probably would have started off with, "what's up, motha licka?' However, it doesn't really feel appropriate today.

"Honey, something has happened," she sighs, her shoulders slumping down and her eyes soften. I try to stay calm, and slowly grab my cup of freshly brewed coffee. I bring it to my lips and blow to cool it down. My mom stares at me, waiting for a response. I'm really uncomfortable in these situations, so I just raised one eyebrow to encourage her to continue. She's silent for a few seconds, but eventually clears her throat. She tucks her dyed blonde hair behind her ear and looks me in the eye.

"Your grandfather... He died last night."

AMANDA: Response Group Reflection

When I was not able to critique the writing I felt lost. I did not know what to say, but as the discussion went on, it become easier to discuss the meaning of the writing rather than critiquing it. In order to get out of my original mindset of critiquing; I looked more at the piece as a whole, analyzing how each of the writer's decisions affected the meaning of the piece. This allowed me to see how beneficial this type of discussion was, because it informed the writer if his overall message was being received.

DYLAN: Draft 2—Response Group 2

Int. CIA Underground Base—day

John tries out his father's occupational name, speaking directly to his father, both confused and excited.

John

A spy... A spy? You're a spy?! Why didn't you tell me sooner? [Shifting to all parents] Why didn't you tell *us* sooner?

Don

When becoming a spy, we're sworn to secrecy.

Robert

We also swore to never have children, but look how that turned out.

Lindsey

We all had beautiful kids. [Turning to her daughter, Jane]
I just wish we never needed to leave you...

David

[Looking at his daughter Kristy] I'm sorry I left you and your mother.

Lisa

We all are sorry for leaving you five and our families, but we had to keep you safe. Our nemesis is among us. We still haven't taken him down.

Sara

He is the one who ordered the attack on you five. He knows about you now and so we had to come back to ensure your safety.

The teenagers look at each other questioning whether the parents planned the speech they just gave, or if they can trust them. Jane takes initiative.

<u>Jane</u>

Okay… So, what do we do? How can we help?

<u>Lindsey</u>

It's not that simple, Jane. You probably don't remember me, or think of me as your mother, but although I left, I love you. I cannot put you – *any* of you - in harm's way… For any reason.

<u>Jane</u>

But we won't be in real danger… Not with these powers.

<u>Robert</u>

Yes, with a little training, you could be extraordinary spies – more so than any other spies in the world, but-

<u>Sara</u>

But we don't know how powerful or dangerous your powers can be… Robert's right, you'd need training. However, we are perfectly capable of finishing this operation on our own.

<u>Lisa</u>

Think of it this way, your powers can act as a defense. If anyone tries to harm any of you again, you can defend yourselves.

<u>John</u>

No. Listen, I want to help out with whatever I can. We can use our powers to secretly follow people, to gather information, and to take people in. We can-

<u>Jane</u>

Spy… I agree. As a team, we could get anything done, absolutely mute. No one would see or hear us at all.

<u>Kristy</u>

We could be your secret weapon. Something that no one sees coming.

<u>Jane</u>

The man who poisoned us believes we're dead. Why not keep it that way? Face it we have an advantage.

<u>Kristy</u>

Ok, so let's vote. Who agrees on us becoming junior spies to help out everyone?

Kristy raises her hand. John and Jane follow. Caleb joins in after debating it a few seconds longer. The four look to Chris who won't even look up at them.

DYLAN: Response Group Reflection

Throughout the reading and annotating of our creative writes, it was interesting when we had to respond with our group members to try to determine the meaning and/or effect that the writer is trying to communicate through their piece—without suggesting any changes or criticism. In this situation, it made me question as to why certain events were occurring, how certain things or lines connect, and even try to determine the writer's deeper meaning.

KRISTEN: Draft 3—Response Group 2

My cheek burns as the cold fall air blows through me. From this height the wind is wild and wreaks havoc on the tall buildings. With my eyes barely open I catch a glimpse of the first morning ray. The sun has become my only source of memory that I have retained from my past life. It wraps the buildings with warmth as it grows endlessly. As the angles of rays expand through the city, the oppression of the night is lifted. As the darkness falls back into the shadows, it reveals the steel buildings unable to move. I sit up and breathe in the air of new beginnings. Stretching my body I stand up in my black suit and watch the morning sun ignite the city. As the rooftop is lightened, I see the man still staring at the door, leading into the unknown inner organs of the building. I walk over to a puddle, caused by the rooftop's many years of neglect, and wash my hair and face. As I dry my face with my black tie, I wander over to the edge of the building and watch as business people rush to their destinations like ants, unable to enjoy the beauty of life.

This morning is no different from the rest of the ones that I have become accustomed to. I walk over to my roof mate and check to see if he is still breathing. And like all of the other days, he sits leaning up against the ledge of the building, watching the door that connects our world to theirs. His eyes are stained with blood by the countless hours of wakefulness. His hair is painted with tints of gray and his face is a blurred shadow of a man. His wrinkles have become permanently implanted on his face. Age spots are sprinkled over his face, revealing his age. His chalky white skin makes him look as if he is dead. He has always looked this way to me since the first day I meet him. But, his absence of speech has just recently become a custom. The first day I arrived he had the stubbornness of a bull, but this drive has faded, just like his voice. That day I woke up to a world of loneliness and denial.

Three months prior, I gasp for air as I feel the pressure of hands around my neck choking me. I am now awake and can hear the screaming of a man on top of me. As I come back into consciousness I see him towering over me. His beard is so long it almost touches my chest. His face is deformed from his wrinkles of anger. His face flames red, while his eyes are bursting out of his face. I put the words together and mumble, "Stop, please stop."

He stares deeply into my fearful eyes, and then suddenly releases me from his grasp. I try to get up, but I am brought to my knees by my body's inability to catch my breath. As I lay coughing on the ground, the man wanders over to the ledge and sits down. When I'm finally able to catch my breath, I approach him trying to regain my manhood. "Who are you? Why am I on top of this roof?"

The man stares at me as if I have insulted his dignity. "Why do you think I attacked you?! I don't why you're up here. I don't even know why I'm up here."

I watched his face as a second of regret flashed over it. "Then let me rephrase my question. Why did you choke me? Who are you?"

"I'm going to have to answer your last question first. I just woke up one day on top of this roof and I haven't been unable to get off of it since. I choked you because I thought you were one of them."

"One of whom?"

"I don't know, but I have a theory." He stops his speech as his eye catches something behind me, but as I turn my head I see nothing.

"Do you see it?" I flinch as I feel his warm breath in my ear. I jump back and watch the man stare at an invisible object floating in the sky.

With caution I ask, "See what?"

He waits a second and says, "The crow right there, sitting on the edge of the building."

"I don't know what…"

"They're watching us I tell you! I keep telling you this why don't you remember? The crow, he torments me." The man moves his eyes as the imaginary bird melts into the sun.

Confused, I ask him, "How could a crow taunt you?"

"He leaves."

"What do you mean he leaves?"

The man steps back a few steps and starts running straight at me. The moment seems to slow down and the man looks determined to attack me. He pushes me to the ground with his arms, as him runs towards the edge of the building. I use my shoulder to absorb the fall as I hit the concrete in pain. I watch him as he jumps right over the edge of the building. I gasp in shock, while I hold my shoulder to get up. I stand up disoriented, stumbling over to the edge of the building. . As I peer over the edge, I watch his body fall to the ground like a rag doll. He hits the ground with the power of a boulder. His body is so implanted into the concrete that I am unable to distinguish where his body ends and the cement begins. I tear my eyes away from the view of his mangled body and try to stabilize my footing. My mind is lost in confusion as I try to regain my composure.

"You're pathetic."

KRISTEN: Response Group Reflection

When we switched from trying to change things about the piece to saying what we noticed, it lightened the conversation. I felt the conversation was more helpful to the author. This also helped us to get the meaning of the piece. It helped the author to see how his/her readers take the piece as a whole.

Notes

1. Page citations for the *Literacies* of *Disciplines* policy research brief map to the original publication of this document, listed in the works cited.

2. This vignette is described with pseudonyms and some conflation.

3. This vignette is described with pseudonyms and some conflation.

4. These conferences were transcribed in 2013 with some conflation.

5. This vignette, described with pseudonyms and some conflation, is based on a 2011 secondary math lab activity.

Annotated Bibliography: Resources and Groups for Going Deeper

Although we found we could generate lengthy lists of resources and groups in multiple disciplines, we thought it might be more helpful to identify a small set of powerful groups and resources that can be "entry ramps" for deeper disciplinary, interdisciplinary, and problem-based work.

Across Disciplines

Buck Institute for Education (BIE)

http://www.bie.org
This national nonprofit is geared toward creating resources and offering sustained-support-model professional learning opportunities around project-based learning. Its website is loaded with video resources and free classroom materials (FreeBIEs), as well as a robust set of research summaries and papers.

Edutopia

http://www.edutopia.org
Edutopia is a large Web interface developed by the George Lucas Educational Foundation to "document . . . disseminate . . . and advocate . . . [for] innovative, replicable, and evidence-based strategies that prepare students to thrive in their future education, careers, and adult lives." The site includes videos, printable guides, and blogs by well-known educators.

MIT OpenCourseWare

http://ocw.mit.edu/index.htm
This collection of more than 2,000 sets of course materials from the Massachusetts Institute of Technology is made available for free through a Web portal. Some of the materials have been organized and even generated specifically for secondary students and their teachers.

National Center for Literacy Education (NCLE)

http://www.literacyinlearningexchange.org/home

NCLE is a coalition of at least thirty professional organizations across disciplines and levels to build capacity and provide support for school-based multidisciplinary teams aiming to strengthen literacy learning within and across disciplines. The website includes video and vignettes featuring work and projects by teams across the nation.

National Writing Project (NWP)

http://www.nwp.org
NWP is a national network of 180+ university–school partnerships serving teachers at all levels and across all disciplines, focusing on "improving the teaching of writing and learning in schools and communities." While the national website is packed with articles and resources, individual sites in all fifty states also have additional resources available through publications, professional development, and the Internet. NWP has also developed a fine Web portal on digital literacies: http://digitalis.nwp.org

New Tech Network (NTN)

http://www.newtechnetwork.org
This is a national network of more than 100 schools implementing a project-based, technology-enhanced, and culture-building approach to learning and teaching. These schools represent some of the most interesting examples of teaching teams and twenty-first-century instruction. The schools' tech plans and templates for instruction could be instructive in a variety of settings.

English Language Arts

Iowa Writers' Workshop

http://www.uiowa.edu/~iww/summer.htm
One of the premiere writing programs in the country holds summer fee-based workshops that are open to members of the public. This opportunity is one of many workshops, institutes, and

conferences teachers could attend to deepen their identities as writers.

New Pages

http://www.newpages.com

This is a Web portal for literary magazines, contests, programs, reviews, and publishers.

Poetry Foundation

http://www.poetryfoundation.org

The foundation's mission is to "celebrate and share the best poetry with the largest audiences through a family of programs." The website is a treasure chest of print and audio poems, video documentaries, and lessons on poetry. The foundation also sponsors the national recitation contest "Poetry Out Loud": http://www.poetry-outloud.org

ReadWriteThink (developed by IRA and NCTE)

http://www.readwritethink.org

This website contains lesson plans and professional development guides for teachers and departments to strengthen the teaching of English language arts.

Mathematics

The Algebra Project

http://www.algebra.org

Founded by civil rights organizer and mathematics educator Bob Moses, this network focuses its efforts on students at the bottom quartile and their teachers, aiming to "raise the floor" through innovative instruction and collaborative partnerships between teachers, mathematicians, mathematics educators, parents, and the students themselves.

Mathematical Association of America (MAA)

http://www.maa.org

A group aimed at "advanc[ing] the mathematical sciences, especially at the collegiate level," MAA conducts professional development, assembles

resources on quantitative reasoning and developmental mathematics, and organizes competitions such as the Mathematical Olympiad Summer Program.

The Math Forum@Drexel

http://mathforum.org/index.html

This is a math center for mathematics and mathematics education based on the Internet and operated by Drexel University. The Math Forum hosts "Ask Dr. Math," Teacher to Teacher exchanges, and Problems of the Week, open-ended, challenging problems and communities to engage with around the solutions and processes developed. The forum also provides professional development through online courses and face-to-face institutes.

National Council of Teachers of Mathematics (NCTM)

http://www.nctm.org

NCTM is a professional organization for mathematics teachers at all levels, "supporting teachers to ensure equitable mathematics learning of the highest quality for all students through vision, leadership, professional development, and research." It hosts conferences, publishes journals, and assembles resources for mathematics teaching. A new website, created by NCTM, illustrates the Common Core State Standards—both mathematical practices and content: http://illuminations.nctm.org

Park City Mathematics Institute (PCMI)

http://pcmi.ias.edu

This is a three-week, intensive national institute held in Park City, Utah, with sessions for mathematicians, advanced mathematics students, mathematics educators, and classroom teachers, sponsored by the Institute of Advanced Study. Even the list of problem sets and technology resources employed at Park City are useful to consider.

Science

Create for STEM Institute

http://www.create4stem.msu.edu
The Create 4 STEM Institute at Michigan State University is a leader in research and support for curriculum and instruction in science and engineering education. The institute is an interdisciplinary collective of leading minds in science, mathematics, and engineering education that engages in educational research to better understand new learning practices, and in the development of curricular and instructional supports for educators to meet the needs of twenty-first-century learners.

The Lawrence Hall of Science (LHS)

http://www.lawrencehallofscience.org
Based at the University of California, Berkeley, the Lawrence Hall of Science has been open for forty-five years with the mission to inspire and develop a learning of science and mathematics. LHS engages in student learning programs ranging from informal activities and resources to developing deep understanding through research-based curriculum and instructional practices. LHS has developed a number of resources for educators that focus on collaborative inquiry learning in science.

National Science Teachers Association (NSTA)

http://www.nsta.org
NSTA is a professional organization for science educators from prekindergarten through college. The organization provides multiple learning supports and programs for educators, focusing on a range of subjects, including questioning and discourse in the science classroom. NSTA provides numerous free resources, as well as a library of resources to members, and offers workshops and networking tools, among other supports.

Next Generation Science Standards (NGSS)

http://www.nextgenscience.org
NGSS is a new set of science performance standards for students that focus on content, practices, and cross-disciplinary understandings. The new standards were developed through a collaborative effort among twenty-six states and science, engineering, and science education professionals and educators. Based on the Framework for K–12 Science Education by the National Research Council, these standards and their supporting documents and resources provide guidance for teaching and learning by focusing on necessary performance outcomes for all students.

Tools for Ambitious Science Teaching: Discourse in the Classroom

http://tools4teachingscience.org
Discourse Tools is one of a system of tools for science educators to develop questioning and discussion practices in the classroom in the broader context of model-based inquiry learning in science. The tools, as well as research-based practices and information, are part of an NSF-funded program at the University of Washington to promote collaborative learning practices in science.

West Hawaii Explorations Academy (WHEA)

http://whea.net/planetwhea/
The charter program in Kona, Hawaii, was developed using the project-based and authentic learning models described in this text, and was founded by one of the leaders of the Konawaena solar car team. Based on the practice of engaging in authentic research in science within its community and ecosystem, this academy uses student-designed projects and investigations of real-world phenomena to engage learners and develop deep understandings of science and other topics.

Social Studies/History

Best of History Websites

http://www.besthistorysites.net
An EdTechTeacher resource, this website portal was created by an experienced history teacher, Tom Daccord, who has worked extensively in a one-to-one computing environment.

Big History Project (BHP)

http://www.bighistoryproject.com

The Big History Project is an innovative, collaborative project aimed at high school students and their teachers. Big history is designed to help students contextualize and connect human science, culture, and history by broadening the focus to the history of the universe, then "zooming" down on particular events, artifacts, or developments. The project is being piloted in schools across the country, and curricular materials are being developed and made accessible online.

National Council for the Social Studies (NCSS)

http://www.socialstudies.org

NCSS is a professional organization for teachers, K–12, teaching "the integrated study of the social sciences and the humanities to promote civic competence." The organization has a variety of supports available, including conferences, professional development sessions, lesson plans, and other resources.

National History Education Clearinghouse (NHEC)

http://teachinghistory.org

The National History Education Clearinghouse is a portal and an online community built around a carefully assembled set of resources for teachers of history K–12. The clearinghouse is funded by the US Department of Education, developed by the Roy Rosenzweig Center for History and New Media, and supported by the American Historical Association.

Technical and Career Education

Association for Career and Technical Education (ACTE)

http://www.acte.org

This national nonprofit education organization focuses on preparing youth and adults for careers. With 25,000 members, ACTE offers professional development, lesson plans, and tools for improving career and technical education. The organization sees student organizations and competitions as essential, so they support a variety of groups, from Business Professionals of America to DECA, HOSA-Future Health Professionals, and SkillsUSA, among others.

International Technology and Engineering Educators Association (ITEEA)

http://www.iteea.org

This professional organization for secondary technology and engineering educators has a membership of 35,000. The organization, established in 1939 to support industrial arts teachers, has evolved significantly within the last thirty years to reflect the impact of technology on all professions and on education.

Bibliography

Allington, R. L. (1980). Teacher interruption behaviors during primary-grade oral reading. *Journal of Educational Psychology, 72*(3), 371–77.

Allington, R. L. (1983a). Fluency: The neglected goal. *The Reading Teacher, 36*(6), 556–61.

Allington, R. L. (1983b). The reading instruction provided readers of differing abilities. *The Elementary School Journal, 83*(5), 548–59.

Allington, R. L. (2006). *What really matters for struggling readers: Designing researched-based programs* (2nd ed.). Boston: Allyn and Bacon.

Applebee, A. N., & Langer, J. A. (2011). A snapshot of writing instruction in middle schools and high schools. *English Journal, 100*(6), 14–27.

Applebee, A. N., Langer, J. A. (with Wilcox, K. C., Nachowitz, M., Mastroianni, M. P., & Dawson, C.). (2013). *Writing instruction that works: Proven methods for middle and high school classrooms.* New York: Teachers College Press; Berkeley: National Writing Project.

Applebee, A. N., Lehr, F., & Auten, A. (1981). Learning to write in the secondary school: How and where. *English Journal, 70*(5), 78–82.

Bailey, C., & Bailey, H. (2014). *Bailey online: A fansite for Chloe and Halle Bailey.* Retrieved from http://chloeandhalle.net

Barron, B., Gomez, K., Pinkard, N., & Martin, C. K. (2014). *The Digital Youth Network: Cultivating digital media citizenship in urban communities.* Cambridge, MA: MIT Press.

Bazerman, C., Little, J., Bethel, L., Chavkin, T., Fouquette, D., & Garufis, J. (2005). *Reference guide to writing across the curriculum.* West Lafayette, IN: Parlor Press; Fort Collins, CO: WAC Clearinghouse.

Bencich, C. B. (1997). Response: A promising beginning for learning to grade student writing. In S. Tchudi (Ed.), *Alternatives to grading student writing* (pp. 47–61). Urbana, IL: National Council of Teachers of English.

Berthoff, A. E. (1981). *The making of meaning: Metaphors, models, and maxims for writing teachers.* Montclair, NJ: Boynton/Cook.

Berthoff, A. E. (Ed.). (1984). *Reclaiming the imagination: Philosophical perspectives for writers and teachers of writing.* Upper Montclair, NJ: Boynton/Cook.

Big History Project. (n.d.). *Teaching Big History.* Retrieved from https://course.bighistoryproject.com/media/homepagemedia/CourseGuide.pdf

Black, P., & Wiliam, D. (1998). Inside the black box: Raising standards through classroom assessment. *Phi Delta Kappan, 80*(2), 139-148.

Black, P., & Wiliam, D. (2004). The formative purpose: Assessment must first promote learning. In M. Wilson (Ed.), *Towards coherence between classroom assessment and accountability* (pp. 20–50). Chicago: National Society for the Study of Education.

Boss, S. (2013, January 3). Learning forum puts PBL teachers on world stage. Retrieved from http://www.edutopia.org/blog/world-stage-project-learning-suzie-boss

Britton, J. (1970). *Language and learning.* Harmondsworth, UK: Penguin.

Buck Institute for Education. (n.d.). http://bie.org

Calkins, L. (1994). *The art of teaching writing* (New Ed.). Portsmouth, NH: Heinemann.

Calkins, L. (2010). *Launch an intermediate writing workshop: Getting started with units of study for teaching writing, grades 3–5.* Portsmouth, NH: Heinemann.

Calkins, L., Hartman, A., & White, Z. (2005). *One to one: The art of conferring with young writers.* Portsmouth, NH: Heinemann.

Carnegie Council on Advancing Adolescent Literacy. (2010). *Time to act: An agenda for advancing adolescent literacy for college and career success.* New York: Carnegie Corporation of New York.

Cary, V. (2004). Working the demand side: An interview with the Algebra Project's Bob Moses. Retrieved from http://www.essentialschools.org/resources/253

Center for Authentic Intellectual Work. (n.d.). http://centerforaiw.com/aiw-framework-and-research

Christie, F., & Maton, K. (2011). Why disciplinarity? In F. Christie & K. Maton (Eds.), *Disciplinarity: Functional linguistic and sociological perspectives* (pp. 1–9). London: Continuum.

Csikszentmihalyi, M. (1990). *Flow: The psychology of optimal experience*. New York: Harper and Row.

Csikszentmihalyi, M. (Feb. 2004). Flow, the secret to Happiness [TED Talk/Video]. Retrieved from http://www.ted.com/talks/mihaly_csikszent mihalyi_on_flow.html

Curtis, C. P. (n.d.). Christopher Paul Curtis. Retrieved from http://www.randomhouse.com/features/christopherpaulcurtis/

Curtis, C. P. (1995). *The Watsons go to Birmingham*. New York: Yearling. (Original work published 1963)

Digital Youth Network. (n.d.). Curriculum. Retrieved May 6, 2014, from www.digitalyouth network.org/12-resources/pages/43-curriculum

Dubinsky, E., & Moses, R. P. (2010). *The Trip Line: A module in the Algebra Project high school curriculum* (student version, Sec. 5, pp. 32). Cambridge, MA: Algebra Project.

Erickson, F. (2004). *Talk and social theory: Ecologies of speaking and listening in everyday life*. Cambridge, UK: Polity Press.

Fulwiler, T. (Ed.). (1987). *The journal book*. Portsmouth, NH: Boynton/Cook.

Gee, J. P. (2004). *Situated language and learning: A critique of traditional schooling*. New York: Routledge.

Gere, A. R. (1985). *Roots in the sawdust: Writing to learn across the disciplines*. Urbana, IL: National Council of Teachers of English.

Gere, A. R., & Shaheen, P. (Eds.). (2001). *Making American literatures in high school and college*. Urbana, IL: National Council Teachers of English.

Google Science Fair. (2013). https://www.google sciencefair.com/en/2013/

Goyal, N. (n.d.) Nikhil Goyal: Kicking bureaucratic ass and taking names. Retrieved from http://nikhilgoyal.me

Goyal, N. (2012). *One size does not fit all: A student's assessment of school* [Kindle]. Retrieved from www.amazon.com/One-Size-Does-Not-Fit/dp/0974525219

Harrison-Barbet, A. W. (Comp.). (2008). Quine: 1908–2000. In *Philosophical Connections*. Retrieved from http://philosophos.org/philosophical_connections/index.html

Hattie, J. (2009). *Visible learning: A synthesis of over 800 meta-analyses relating to achievement*. New York: Routledge.

Hattie, J. (2012). *Visible learning for teachers: Maximizing impact on learning*. New York: Routledge.

Hicks, T. (2013). *Crafting digital writing: Composing texts across media and genres*. Portsmouth, NH: Heinemann.

ImaginationNation Matters. (n.d.). Retrieved from http://imagine.icsmich.org/

Koch, R. (1982). Syllogisms and superstitions: The current state of responding to writing. *Language Arts, 59*(5), 464–471.

Langer, J. A. (2011). *Envisioning knowledge: Building literacy in the academic disciplines*. New York: Teachers College Press.

McKean, L. E.. (2013). *Critical response process protocol* (adapted from *Critical response process* by Liz Lerman). Bloomington, IN: National School Reform Faculty. Retrieved from http://www.nsrfharmony.org/connections/CriticalResponseProcess Adaptation.pdf

Mehlinger, H. (1995). *School reform in the information age*. Bloomington: Indiana University Press.

Moje, E. B. (2007). Developing socially just subject-matter instruction: A review of the literature on disciplinary literacy teaching. *Review of Research in Education, 31*, 1–44.

Moje, E. B. (2008). Foregrounding the disciplines in secondary literacy teaching and learning: A call for change. *Journal of Adolescent and Adult Literacy, 52*(2), 96–107.

Moje, E. B. (2011). Developing disciplinary discourses, literacies, and identities: What's knowledge got to do with it? In G. López-Bonilla & K. Englander (Eds.), *Discourses and identities in contexts of educational change: Contributions from the United States and Mexico* (pp. 49–74). New York: Peter Lang.

Monroy, C. (2011). Caine's arcade: A cardboard arcade made by a 9-year old boy. Retrieved from http://cainesarcade.com

Moses, R. P., & Cobb, C. E., Jr. (2001). *Radical equations: Civil rights from Mississippi to the Algebra Project.* Boston: Beacon Press.

Moses, R. P., West, M. M., & Davis, F. D. (2009). Culturally responsive education in the Algebra Project. In B. Greer, S. Mukhopadhyay, A. B. Powell, & S. Nelson-Barber (Eds.), *Culturally responsive mathematics education* (pp. 239–256). New York: Routledge.

National Board of Professional Teaching Standards. (n.d.). http://www.nbpts.org/members-learning-communities

National Council of Teachers of English, James R. Squire Office of Policy Research. (2011). Literacies *of* disciplines. *Council Chronicle 21*(1), 15–18.

National Research Council. (2000). *How people learn: Brain, mind, experience, and school* (Expanded ed.). Washington, DC: National Academies Press.

National Research Council. (2012). *A framework for K–12 science education: Practices, crosscutting concepts, and core ideas.* Washington, DC: National Academies Press.

National Writing Project. (n.d.). *Guidelines for response groups.* Handout from NWP Writing and Technology: A Professional Writing Retreat, Nebraska City, NE. Retrieved from http://www.nwp.org/cs/public/download/nwp_file/12381/Guidelines_for_Response_Groups.pdf?x-r=pcfile_d

Newmann, F. M., Secada, W. G., & Wehlage, G. G. (1995). *A guide to authentic instruction and assessment: Vision, standards, and scoring.* Madison: Wisconsin Center for Education Research.

Newmann, F. M., & Wehlage, G. G. (1993). Five standards of authentic instruction. *Educational Leadership, 50*(7), 8–12.

Next Generation Science Standards. (n.d.). Retrieved from http://www.nextgenscience.org

New Tech Network. (n.d.). http://www.newtechnetwork.org

Owocki, G., & Goodman, Y. (2002). *Kidwatching: Documenting children's literacy development.* Portsmouth, NH: Heinemann.

Palincsar, A. S. (1982). *Improving the reading comprehension of junior high students through the reciprocal teaching of comprehension-monitoring strategies* (Unpublished doctoral dissertation). University of Illinois at Urbana-Champaign.

Palincsar, A. S., & Brown, A. L. (1984). Reciprocal teaching of comprehension-fostering and comprehension-monitoring activities. *Cognition and Instruction, 1*(2), 117–75.

Parker, J. (2002). A new disciplinarity: Communities of knowledge, learning, and practice. *Teaching in Higher Education, 7*(4), 373–86.

Pearson P. D., & Fielding, L. (1991). Comprehension instruction. In R. Barr, M. L. Kamil, P. B. Mosenthal, & P. D. Pearson (Eds.), *Handbook of reading research* (Vol. II, pp. 815–60). New York: Longman.

Pearson, P. D., & Gallagher, M. C. (1983). The instruction of reading comprehension. *Contemporary Educational Psychology, 8*(3), 317–44.

Pearson, P. D., & Johnson, D. D. (1978). *Teaching reading comprehension.* New York: Holt, Rinehart and Winston.

Popham, W. J. (2008). *Transformative assessment.* Alexandria, VA: ASCD.

Pressley, M., & Afflerbach, P. (1995). *Verbal protocols of reading: The nature of constructively responsive reading.* Hillsdale, NJ: Erlbaum.

Pressley, M., Almasi, J., Schuder, T., Bergman, J., Hite, S., El-Dinary, P. B., & R. Brown. (1994). Transactional instruction of comprehension strategies: The Montgomery County, Maryland, SAIL Program. *Reading and Writing Quarterly: Overcoming Learning Difficulties, 10*(1), 5–19.

Pressley, M., El-Dinary, P. B., Gaskins, I., Schuder, T., Bergman, J. L., Almasi, J., & R. Brown. (1992). Beyond direct explanation: Transactional instruction of reading comprehension strategies. *The Elementary School Journal, 92*(5), 513–55.

Reeves, T. C., Herrington, C., & Oliver, R. (2002). Authentic activities and online learning. In *Quality conversations, proceedings of the 25th HERDSA annual conference.* Perth, Western Australia: Higher Education Research and Development Society of Australasia.

Russell, D. (2009). Bob Moses and the Algebra Project. In D. Russell (Ed.), *Black genius: Inspirational portraits of America's black leaders* (pp. 326–343). New York: Skyhorse.

Shanahan, T., & Shanahan, C. (2012). What is disciplinary literacy and why does it matter? *Topics in Language Disorders, 32*(1), 7–18.

Shayer, M. (2003). Not just Piaget; not just Vygotsky, and certainly not Vygotsky as *alternative* to Piaget. *Learning and Instruction, 13*(5), 465–485.

Tomasello, M. (1999). *The cultural origins of human cognition.* Cambridge, MA: Harvard University Press.

Wiggins, G. (2012, Jan. 11). Transfer as the point of education. Retrieved from http://grantwiggins .wordpress.com/2012/01/11/transfer-as-the-point-of-education/

Wilhelm, J. D., Baker, T. N., & Dube, J. (2001). *Strategic reading: Guiding students to lifelong literacy, 6–12.* Portsmouth, NH: Boynton/Cook.

Williamson, J. (Ed.). (2003). *Design writing 2: Cities, design, and democracy.* Bloomfield Hills MI: Cranbrook Academy of Art.

Wineburg, S. S. (1991). On the reading of historical texts: Notes on the breach between school and academy. *American Educational Research Journal, 28*(3), 495–519.

Wineburg, S. S., Martin, D., & Monte-Sano, C. (2013). *Reading like a historian: Teaching literacy in middle and high school history classrooms.* New York: Teachers College Press.

Young, A., & Fulwiler, T. (Eds.). (1986). *Writing across the disciplines: Research into practice.* Upper Montclair, NJ: Boynton/Cook

Yousafzai, M. (n.d.). http://malalafund.org

Yousafzai, M. (with Lamb, C.). (2013). *I am Malala: The girl who stood up for education and was shot by the Taliban.* New York: Little, Brown.

Zemelman, S., Daniels, H., & Hyde, A. (2012). *Best practice: Bring standards to life in America's classrooms.* Portsmouth, NH: Heinemann.

Index

Authors

Linda Denstaedt is a literacy consultant and co-director of the Oakland Writing Project (MI). In 2002 she retired from teaching high school English and facilitating staff learning for Clarkston Community Schools as director of writing. She currently works alongside teachers in and out of classrooms at Oak Park High School, a high-priority school bordering Detroit. Denstaedt collaboratively coaches teachers to become students of themselves and their students as they develop units of study, instructional practices, and formative assessments to accelerate student learning. She also serves on the National Writing Project i3 College-Ready Writers Program Leadership Team, which supports a national professional learning program for rural teachers focused on improving student writing. These collaborations lead to identifying strategic ways teachers and students can make change in challenging lives, classrooms, and times.

Laura Jane Roop is the new director of the Western Pennsylvania Writing Project and is an assistant professor at the University of Pittsburgh. Previously, she directed the Oakland Writing Project and worked as school research-relations coordinator at the University of Michigan–Ann Arbor. Roop spans boundaries, networking with university researchers, practicing teachers, and representatives from community organizations to establish generative networks for professional learning. She is interested in multiple literacies and in redressing inequities for students of color and students living in poverty. She is also a practicing poet who has learned from that genre how to lean out into "what could be" in terms of texts and institutions. Roop won the Richard Meade Award for Research in English Language Arts Education with her colleagues Anne Ruggles Gere, Colleen Fairbanks, Alan Howes, and David Schaafsma for *Language and Reflection: An Integrated Approach to Teaching English* (1992).

Stephen Best currently directs programs in curriculum and instruction, school improvement, and educational technology for the Michigan Department of Education. Before this, he led research and curriculum initiatives in STEM fields at the University of Michigan and led several teacher education programs and outreach efforts. Best began his work in education as a mathematics and science teacher in Michigan and Hawaii. He is married with two children and a house full of pets in west Michigan.

This book was typeset in Janson Text and BotonBQ by
Barbara Frazier.

Typefaces used on the cover include American Typewriter,
Frutiger Bold, Formata Light, and Formata Bold.

The book was printed on 60-lb. White Recycled Offset paper
by Versa Press, Inc.

30% Total Recycled Fiber